Murder, Media, and Metamorphosis

John D'Amico

Published by John D'Amico, 2024.

MURDER, MEDIA, AND METAMORPHOSIS

First edition. May 31, 2024.

Copyright © 2024 John D'Amico.

ISBN: 979-8224623778

Written by John D'Amico.

Table of Contents

I dedicate this book to my wife Sandy and daughter Kimberly for their love, patience, and support that made my public service career and this book possible.

Introduction

———

This book is a memoir and a guidebook to save American democracy and the planet. The title *Murder, Media, and Metamorphosis* reflects my career journey and how print media led me to public service. I talk about the significance of current and future generations tackling social and environmental issues I confronted that remain unresolved: global warming, pollution, overdevelopment, overfishing, waste mismanagement, recycling, crime, family dissolution, homelessness, racism, nuclear hazards, and the assault on democracy. To prevent the enemies of the Constitution from unraveling our republic and humankind from destroying our terrestrial home, we must revive the community spirit and social commitment that prevailed before the advent of cell phones and social media. I use my experience to suggest ways you, your family, relatives, friends, fellow citizens, and elected officials throughout the country and the world can and must address these challenges.

My ancestry traces back to one of the most beautiful villages in Italy. My father's life and his hometown, Montalbano Elicona, encompass a microcosm of the history of Sicily and a slice of American history. 8th and 7th Century Greek colonists added the name "Elicona" to "Montalbano" because it resembled the Greek Mt. Helicon, where Narcissus was inspired by his own beauty as reflected in the water. In the Roman era, the legions of Octavian, the future Ceasar Augustus, defeated Sextus Pompeius, the son of Pompey the Great, in Montalbano. In the 1200's Holy Roman Emperor Frederick II of Swabia built a castle on top of Montalbano. Nietzsche called him the first European, and historians regard him as the first modern ruler.

At age 17, my father left Montalbano Elicona so he could provide for his poor family. A member of a small group of young men recruited and funded by the Mafia, he was the only one to make it to America. The mob reluctantly accepted his refusal to join its ranks. He became a US citizen, later owning and operating successful beauty salons in New Jersey. He married Elvira Caravello, whose parents migrated from Palermo to Brooklyn, New York, and they raised three children, of which I was the oldest. Despite not advancing past grammar school, my parents stressed the value of education, urged us to study hard, and encouraged us to be productive members of society. It paid off. They proudly attended our graduations from prestigious colleges and universities, and they enjoyed the highlights of my marriage, career, and public service.

The "murder" theme in my work relates to my legal and political careers, starting with a connection to two well-known murders in New Jersey. Nationally famous attorney F. Lee Bailey represented the defendant in one of them. I explain in my last four chapters how the specter of murder has returned to threaten our planet and American democracy.

"Media" describes how honest and reputable local newspapers helped me, fellow members of the Irate Shore Commuters, and others improve the quality of life for state residents. They fueled a revolt by rush hour radicals that prevented the demise of commuter rail service and led to the formation of New Jersey Transit. This story shows how citizens who do not usually get involved in politics can come together and make the government address critical issues that affect their lives. Traditional media's detailed reporting and editorials helped me win election to the Oceanport Borough Council, Monmouth County Board of County Commissioners, and New Jersey State Senate.

"Metamorphosis" represents my career changes and spiritual growth, leading to a positive impact on others. The largest life insurance company failure in United States history ended my 21-year corporate legal career. I helped the New Jersey Insurance Commissioner hold the directors and officers of The Mutual Benefit Life Insurance Company accountable for excessive and unprofitable real estate investments, managerial incompetence, and self-dealing. I warn corporate directors about their responsibilities, like duty of care and loyalty, and give examples of recent failures by directors at Fox News and fossil fuel companies.

My political achievements helped me become a judge in the Superior Court of New Jersey after leaving Mutual Benefit Life. In the Family Division. I presided over divorces, domestic violence, child abuse and neglect, alimony, child support, equitable distribution, and termination of parental rights. I share perspectives on the challenge of deciding such matters and offer ancient wisdom for people experiencing family difficulties. During my time in the Civil Division, I introduced a more efficient way of conducting jury trials called the "Expedited Jury Trial." This method saves time and money by using documents and expert reports instead of live testimony. New Jersey uses it frequently, and other states, including California and Florida, have emulated it. I offer reasons New Jersey's judiciary has an excellent nationwide reputation and suggest that other states adopt New Jersey's system of appointing judges instead of electing them. I also recommend that they and the US Supreme Court promulgate ethics rules patterned after the exemplary New Jersey Supreme Court Code of Judicial Conduct.

Following retirement from the bench, the Governor appointed me Chair of the New Jersey State Parole Board with a mandate to rid the agency of scandal and reform its policies and procedures. My research on crime causes and the problems of prisoner reintegration led to reforms that have reduced recidivism rates. Paroling authorities nationwide should take note. The Parole Board curtailed parole revocations because of technical violations. It implemented a parole program that relied on evidence and used tools to assess risk and needs. It also used incentives and penalties to motivate parole compliance. Parole Board Community Partnership Conferences held in the state's major cities motivated ministers and faith-based organizations to adopt "faith-based" substance abuse counseling ministries that are contributing to the spiritual metamorphosis of parolees. I discuss the key role they can play in the war on drugs in Chapter 8.

The conferences also produced task forces composed of community groups, charitable organizations, religious leaders, and concerned citizens that are helping parolees deal with physical and mental illness, lack of education, sexual predation, employment, housing, and transportation. States should follow New Jersey's lead in implementing administrative parole procedures to lower the prison population. They should also mandate parole supervision for all inmates upon leaving prison to prevent crime and ensure successful prisoner re-entry.

I was content to spend my retirement from the Parole Board serving on the Boards of two non-profit entities and playing golf. I had no intention of doing the arduous work of authoring a book. All that changed on January 6, 2021. The mob invasion of the US Capitol to prevent the peaceful transfer of presidential power shocked me into the realization that the constitutional republic that had done so much for my family is very fragile and might not survive. I also fear that humankind is committing global murder/suicide. Antagonists like the fossil fuel industry and global warming and climate change deniers, abetted by an ill-informed and torpid citizenry, are mounting a murderous assault on the earth and its waters.

Beginning in 2010, social media irrevocably altered national and local politics. The shift to social media and right-wing media ended my political career and is now endangering the planet. Climate deniers have set back efforts to address the consequences of global warming. I discuss the steps governments at all levels in the United States and around the world must take to combat the perils of climate change, including drought, water shortages, wildfires, hurricanes, flooding, rising sea levels, and economic impacts.

I also discuss the urgency of dealing with water pollution. I chair the NY/NJ Baykeeper, an organization focused on revitalizing the Hudson/Raritan Estuary. Our efforts include suing polluters, restoring oysters, controlling pollution, reducing sewer outflows, and addressing plastic pollution. These programs are steps governments should undertake locally, nationally, and internationally to defend the waters of the earth and keep our own bodies clean. The United States is the richest nation in the world and must lead and fund the efforts required to prevent the murder of the planet. This can only happen, however, if American democratic institutions remain strong.

Modern social media platforms, like Instagram, Facebook, X, and Snapchat, have useful and fun features. However, they also empower radical individuals and fringe groups, like Q-Anon, to control and divide our national conversation. Additionally, they facilitate foreign intervention in our elections and support those who deny election results, endangering American democracy. Meaningful regulation of social media excesses is not imminent. We must therefore educate young students about media literacy to help them avoid the toxic influences of xenophobia, neo-Nazism, racism, misogyny, antisemitism, and authoritarianism.

We should have stronger civics education. My 11th grade teacher insisted that I learn and understand the basic principles of American democracy. Americans should know and appreciate the historical and philosophical foundations of our republic. Citizens should support policies and candidates that protect the Constitution and insure the positive metamorphosis of American government. My advice to you, the reader, is to determine what stirs your passion. Study the issues you care about and join, support, and contribute to the organizations mentioned in the text and footnotes that share your concerns.

There are many books about the subjects I cover. None of them, including this one, are new. The authors of the books of the Bible covered these topics 2,000 years ago. In his *Autobiography* Benjamin Franklin said we should "imitate Jesus and Socrates." Throughout my life and in this writing, I have attempted to heed Franklin's advice by asking questions and seeking the truth like Socrates. I have also embraced the teachings of Jesus, who showed unwavering devotion to love and sacrificed his life for it. I therefore cite the Bible to show how Jesus, his apostles, and the Old Testament prophets gave us teachings and warnings pertinent to today's problems. We ignore them at our peril.

Chapter 1: Montalbano Elicona

Children, obey your parents in the Lord, for this is right. Honor your father and mother, which is the first commandment with promise: that it may be well with you, and you may live long on the earth. [1]

—-*Ephesians 6:1-3*

MY FATHER, GIOVANNI D'Amico, was born in Montalbano Elicona, Sicily, in 1905. His mother, Fiore Collichio, was of Greek ancestry. Her father made Sicilian bagpipes. The Italian bagpipe, made of reeds and a sheep's hide, dates to the time of Roman Emperor Nero. Christmastime bagpipe-blowing shepherds traditionally come down from nearby Mount Etna to play in the villages. My paternal grandfather was a forest ranger charged with protecting the Sicilian fruit and nut orchards of King Umberto I (1870-1900) and King Victor Emmanuel III (1900-1946). The D'Amico family was poor but able to nurture Giovanni and his two sisters, Francesca, and Gina. Gina died in childbirth. Her son Vincenzo (Enzo) was my only Italian first cousin.

My father vaguely remembered being shaken in his carriage by the great Messina earthquake of 1908, in which 80,000 people died. He attended school through the sixth grade. He and his classmates often played hooky from school, hiding among ancient megalithic stones of unknown origin on a plateau a short walk from the village called Argimusco. Specialists believe this was a place of worship for primitive peoples, or even a magical site whose symbols referred to the constellations. Others maintain they are simply a natural formation.

Italians applaud Montalbano Elicona as one of the most beautiful villages in Italy. It encompasses a microcosm of the history of Sicily and a slice of American history. A majestic castle crowns the medieval village, which is surrounded by millennial forests. With a population of 2,500, it borders an ancient Roman road between the Mediterranean and Ionian coasts of north-eastern Sicily. Perched on a mountain at an elevation of 3,000 feet, it offers an incredible view of the smoking Etna volcano thirteen miles to the south. On the other side are splendid views of the Aeolian Islands.

The name "Montalbano" means "white mountain." Scholars also link it to the Arabic word "al-bana," meaning "excellent place." The Greeks who colonized Sicily in the 8th and 7th centuries, B.C., noted its similarity to the Greek mountain called "Helicon." Both towns share the same elevation and a stream and river that meanders tortuously through to an adjacent valley. In Greek mythology, there were two springs sacred to the Muses at Helicon. One of them burst from a spot forcefully struck by the hoof of the winged horse Pegasus. In the other, the beauty of his reflection in the water inspired Narcissus. The waterways of Montalbano thus got the name "Elicona," which is Italian for "Helicon."

In the Roman era, Sextus Pompeius, the son of Pompey the Great, seized Sicily and its sea routes. Octavian vied with Pompey for power and tried to appease Sextus Pompeius by marrying one of his relatives. The marriage quickly ended in divorce based on irreconcilable differences. War soon followed. In 36 AD, Octavian's legions united with other militia forces at Agrimusco. They launched a decisive attack that forced Pompeius to retreat to Messina and take to sea. Using a fleet borrowed from Mark Anthony, Octavian's schoolmate Marcus Agrippa defeated Pompeius. Octavian later became Rome's first great emperor, Caesar Augustus.

In the 1190s, Emperor Henry VI took Sicily from the Normans. When he died in 1197, his southwest German house of Hohenstaufen and the rival house of the Guelfs disputed his succession to the empire. The Hohenstaufen, in the person of Henry VI's widow, Constance, held on to Sicily with papal help. In 1198, Pope Innocent III assumed control of Sicily as the guardian of Constance's infant son Frederick, later known as Frederick II of Swabia. In 1211. The pope conferred on him the title of "Holy Roman Emperor." The same year, the pope ratified the gift of Montalbano given by Frederick II to Constance of Aragon, with all its residences and tenements. Thus, Montalbano became part of the royal domain.

Professor Donald Detwiler describes Frederick II as "a man of extraordinary culture, energy, and ability—called by a contemporary chronicler, *stupor mundi,* the wonder of the world, by Nietzsche the first European, and by many historians the first modern ruler. Frederick II established in Sicily and southern Italy something very much like a modern, centrally governed kingdom with an efficient bureaucracy." [2] He maintained and deepened religious toleration, giving freedom of worship to Muslims and Jews. Able to speak six languages (Latin, Sicilian, German, French, Greek, and Arabic), he was an avid patron of science and the arts. He also played a leading role in promoting literature through the Sicilian School of poetry, which had a major influence on what was to become the modern Italian language.

Angered by a Guelf rebellion in 1233, Frederick II destroyed Montalbano and deported its inhabitants. Soon thereafter, however, he recognized its strategic value at the crossroads between the Ionic and Tyrrhenian Seas and as a gateway to the interior of Sicily, and he strengthened its fortifications. He built a castle on top of the mountain on preexisting Byzantine and Arab structures and gave the fortress to his wife, Constance of Aragon.

The next ruler with substantial connections to Montalbano was Frederick III of Aragon. In 1302, the Treaty of Calabellotta ended the 20 years of rebellion against French colonization. The rebellion, called the "Sicilian Vespers," is the subject of Giuseppe Verdi's opera "I Vespri Siciliani." Frederick III ruled the kingdom until his death in 1337. He transformed Montalbano castle from a fortress to a royal summer residence. While there, his trusted personal physician, Arnaldo da Villanova, treated his gout.

Frederick III organized the Sicilian parliament into an assembly of three houses modeled after the three estates of the kingdom of Aragon. They represented the feudal landowners, the clergy, and the towns of the royal domain. From the castle of Montalbano in 1311, he issued the oldest rules in Europe for the election of administrative officials in the city of Palermo. In 1805, Montalbano passed into the hands of the Society of Jesus. After Italian reunification in the 1860s, the government confiscated ecclesiastic properties, and Montalbano became a municipality.

In 1967, my father returned to his native land with our entire family. We toured Turin, Venice, Florence and Rome with my Aunt Franca and my cousin Enzo and visited Montalbano. By then, King Frederick II's castle was in ruins. There were cows and chickens in the streets, and the authorities shut off the water every night at 8 PM. The only shabby hotel in town housed a movie theater in the basement. I had trouble sleeping there because of the screaming and cheering of the audience as it watched a "Godzilla" movie. My father wanted to buy property in Montalbano and build a modern hotel. We persuaded him not to pursue his plan. Of course, it turned out that he was right. Montalbano restored the castle in the 1980s, and tourists can now stay at the four-star Hotel Federico II for €138 a night.

Conditions were much worse in Montalbano in 1922, the year Benito Mussolini came to power. My father therefore agreed to lead a small group of young men on a perilous journey from Sicily to America, funded by the Mafia. His aim was to find work in the new world and send money back to his struggling family. Arrests and injuries decimated the group as it moved north through Italy. Many returned home. My father was the only member to reach the French border. Chased by a border guard, he escaped into France by throwing his suitcase at the guard's feet, causing him to fall. He sailed out of Le Havre and disembarked at Ellis Island at age 17, unable to speak English and with only $6 in his pocket. He entered the United States just in time. The Immigration Act of 1924 favored immigrants from northern Europe and imposed strict quotas on Southern Europeans.

He found work as a barber in New York City. One day, a well-dressed customer asked him for a haircut and gave him a tip of $5, a week's income in the 1920s. After the second and third haircut and tip, my father inquired about this special treatment. The customer replied he was a Mafia messenger who wanted my father to join the organization and smuggle narcotics between Sicily and New York. My father said he was not interested in the job. The Mafioso refused to take "no" for an answer and threatened physical harm. My father replied that he owned a gun and was prepared to defend himself. The mob backed off, and my father followed through with his original intention, which was to support himself honestly and send money to his poor family in Italy. He did so for the rest of his life.

In 1928, Giovanni drove to California with a business partner named Albert Carlozzo, also from Sicily, and opened a beauty salon in Hollywood. Their clientele included aspiring actors and rising stars. Unfortunately, Albert had impregnated his girlfriend in New Jersey. Motivated by the ancient Sicilian code of honor, my father closed the shop and drove Albert back to the East Coast so that he could marry the woman in question.

Dad became a US citizen and established successful beauty shops in Red Bank, NJ named "John's Beauty Salon." In 1939, his barber Vincent Cannamela introduced him to a lovely young girl from Brooklyn named Elvira Caravello. Her parents had migrated from Palermo, had experienced tough times during the Depression, and had passed away by the time she turned twenty-one. The youngest of nine Caravello children, she went to Perth Amboy, New Jersey, to live with her sister Mary and her husband Anthony Cannamela. Tony's brother Vincent Cannamela was married to her sister Clara, and his other brother Frank was married to her sister Stella. All three brothers immigrated from Sicily. They were co-owners of the American Barber Shop in Perth Amboy. The three families lived in a large house divided into four apartments, and they shared the rent from the fourth apartment three ways. This unusual scenario was featured in *Ripley's Believe it or Not.*

John and Elvira married in 1940. I was born on January 24, 1941, my sister Anita on May 31, 1944, and my brother Victor on July 10, 1949. My earliest memory dates to August 14, 1945, V-J Day, or Victory over Japan Day, marking the end of World War II, the deadliest and most destructive war in history. When President Harry S. Truman announced that Japan had surrendered unconditionally, war-weary citizens around the world erupted in celebration. What impressed me as I sat on my father's shoulders was the noise of passing cars blowing their horns and dragging tin cans from their rear bumpers. I thank the "greatest generation" for fighting and winning the war and saving the world from authoritarian fascism.

When we were young, we would often visit our aunts and uncles in Perth Amboy, New Jersey. My Uncle Vincent, whose son Vincent Jr. became a doctor, urged me to educate myself by reading New York Times editorials and Time magazine. He also introduced me to the wonderful world of Italian opera. Like my uncle Vincent, my father was highly intelligent. A self-taught philosopher who gave psychological advice to his customers, he authored articles in a local newspaper and spoke on local radio about physical and mental health and inner youth and beauty. "Deepak Chopra" ahead of his time. His favorite saying was "as you think, so shall you be." Although he left school after the sixth grade, he was smart enough to seek advice from his customers. At a teacher's suggestion, he forced all three of us to take piano lessons to develop good study habits. His insistence on daily practice did the trick but led to many arguments and reprimands. On one occasion, when visiting, relatives asked me to play a song on the piano, I expressed my frustrations by playing "Nobody Knows the Trouble I've Seen."

The piano lessons produced the desired effect. Anita, Vic, and I all studied hard and got good grades. Mom and Dad stressed the virtue of hard work. They made it clear that we should treat everyone with respect, regardless of their race, ancestry, sex, ethnicity, or creed. Beyond that, was the mandate to be good persons and citizens. Unspoken but understood was the expectation that we would enjoy better, more prosperous, and more productive careers and lives than my father and mother had endured. I applied these lessons during my years at Red Bank High School. I got excellent grades, was consistently on the Honor Roll and became the President of the school's National Honor Society chapter. I won my first election in the spring of my junior year. My classmates elected me Senior Class President by a five-vote margin over a popular athlete who had rebuked his baseball team a few days earlier for losing a game while he was on the mound trying to impress scouts in the stands. All but one of my future elections would also be close.

My parents were not churchgoers except on major holidays. Just before I got too old to enroll, they sent me to St. Anthony's Catholic Church in Red Bank for catechism and confirmation classes. I was significantly older than the rest of the class, which included my future wife. Just before confirmation, the Mother Superior asked the class for the name of the bishop who would be coming. All hands went up except mine, so the nun called on me. I did not know the answer. The nun's response was, "the big ones are stupider than the little ones." We had to attend confession before confirmation. During my session with the priest, I admitted I did not attend mass regularly because my parents did not take me to church. His response was to yell at me as if my parents' dereliction was my fault. Because of this unfortunate experience, it would be years before regular church attendance would become part of my life. To his credit, however, my father urged me to study the gospel of Matthew. He emphasized Chapter 22:37-39: "... You shall love the Lord your God with all your heart, with all your soul, and with all your mind. This is the first commandment. And the second is like it: You shall love your neighbor as yourself." This advice would serve me well in later years.

I am grateful to Montalbano Elicona and my ancestors for nurturing Giovanni D'Amico and launching him on his marvelous adventure. I am also extremely grateful to the country of my birth, the United States of America, and for the opportunities it afforded our family. Since the founding of the nation, immigrants have played a vital role in creating a diverse, dynamic, and growing economy. Immigrants make up more than a third of the workforce in some industries. By being flexible with where they live, they help local economies manage worker shortages. Immigrant workers support the aging native-born

US population by boosting the number of workers and reinforcing Social Security and Medicare funds. Children born to immigrant families are upwardly mobile, promising future benefits not only to their families, but to the US economy overall.[3] The bottom line is we need more immigration to augment the population and help the US remain globally competitive.

I praise and honor my parents for all they have done for my sister, brother, and me. Although labeled "stupid" by the Mother Superior at St. Anthony's Church, I heeded my parents' insistence that I study hard and get good grades. It paid off. I was the first person in the family to graduate from high school. I suppressed my tears with a grateful smile when my parents attended my graduations from Harvard College and Harvard Law School.

It had been an exciting time to be a college student. John F. Kennedy exploited television to win election to the Presidency in 1960. We had high hopes for a brighter future in America. Before his Inauguration, the President-elect returned to his *alma mater* to attend a meeting of the Harvard College Board of Overseers. I was among hundreds of students who watched him ascend the steps of University Hall. We yelled "speech! Speech!" and he turned around. He said, "I am going to talk to President Pusey about your grades." We groaned. He smiled broadly, raised his arm, and replied, "I will represent your interests." We cheered not only on that occasion, but also a year and a half later when he attended a football game. The band, of which my roommate Dr. Harry Knopf was a member, played "Hail to the Chief" as he took his seat. At halftime, the band played "Hit the Road Jack" and Kennedy left. We would not see him again.

I was in law school when the President was assassinated on November 22, 1963, I walked the campus in stunned silence as church bells all over Cambridge marked the somber occasion. What followed were turbulent years of war in Vietnam, riots, battles over civil rights and poverty, and the murder of the Reverend Dr. Martin Luther King, Jr., and Robert Kennedy. Murder would also predominate during my first year as an attorney.

Chapter 2: Murder

———

Truly, the hearts of the sons of men are full of evil; madness is in their hearts while they live, and after that they go to the dead.

—-Ecclesiastes 9:3

"This is not a murder case at all," said nationally renowned attorney F. Lee Bailey in his summation. "It is something that was dreamed up—something that never happened." But the trial did happen at the Monmouth County Courthouse. I had just graduated from law school, passed the New Jersey bar examination, and been sworn in as an attorney. Monmouth County Court judges Thomas J. Smith and Edward Ascher had appointed me as their law clerk. I never imagined that during my one-year term in their employ I would witness the performance of the greatest criminal defense attorney of the twentieth century and do legal work on one of New Jersey's most infamous murder trials.

Judge Smith had just begun handling criminal motions and trials. In the fall of 1966, he presided over his first murder trial. It would be a preliminary skirmish before the main event. The State of New Jersey accused Edward Lynch of murdering Mrs. Dorothy McKenzie, mother of four children. He allegedly shot her in the head twice at close range with a 33-caliber pistol. Monmouth County Prosecutor Vincent P Keuper represented the State. Attorney Joseph Mattice represented the defendant.

While bartending in the Town Tavern, Toms River, New Jersey, Lynch had spilled ice on McKenzie's lap. She was upset and told Lynch he was no bartender, never was a bartender, and that "you are finished." Lynch told an acquaintance that he was "mad" at Mrs. McKenzie because she wanted to cause him trouble and had telephoned him frequently at the bar and at his home. Prosecutor Keuper elicited testimony from Lynch's drinking buddy, quoting Lynch as saying, "Bill, I did it. I bumped Dotty off." Lynch testified the gun went off accidentally when Mrs. McKenzie threatened him with it. Prosecutor

Keuper argued that Lynch planned the murder and deserved the death penalty. During his emotional summation in defense of Lynch, Mattice employed a trick for which he was famous at the courthouse. To wipe sweat off his forehead, he yanked his handkerchief out of his suit pocket, causing a set of rosary beads to fall to the floor in front of the jury. To no avail. The jury convicted Lynch of unpremeditated second-degree murder.

Judge Smith and I worked overtime and, on a Saturday, to draft his instructions to the jury. On the last day of the trial, the Judge carefully read his charge to the jury and thanked me for my help. He then told the jury that he had put a lot of time preparing the charge so that the record would be accurate and complete "in the event of an appeal." I buried my head in my hands as Mr. Mattice sprang to his feet to move for a mistrial. He argued that the Judge's comment suggested to the jury that it should convict his client. Judge Smith denied the motion and sentenced Lynch to 25-30 years in state prison. There was no appeal.

Thus ended a preliminary skirmish before the main event, the twentieth century's greatest legal battle in the Monmouth County Courthouse. Before 1966, the last major battle near Freehold, then called Monmouth Court House, occurred on a hot June day in 1778. France's promise of military aid to the American Revolution caused British forces to leave Philadelphia for New York. Baron Friedrich Wilhelm von Steuben had trained Washington's army during the winter at Valley Forge. As a result, General George Washington did not hesitate to attack the British in Monmouth County while they were resting. General Charles Lee commanded the American forces, but his slow movements allowed British General Sir Henry Clinton to get ready for a fight. As Washington approached the battlefield with the main American Army, he encountered Lee and his troops in retreat. He took command after a stern, expletive-filled rebuke of Lee, and rallied his forces. British assaults failed to dislodge the Americans, so General Clinton withdrew and proceeded to New York. Both sides suffered heavy casualties, caused as much by the 100-degree heat and fatigue as by gunfire. The Battle of Monmouth was the last major engagement in the north, and with 26,000 soldiers engaged, one of the largest of the Revolutionary War. Historians say it was a draw, but Washington considered it a victory because his army matched the skills of a British army reputed to be the best in the world.

In December 1966, Monmouth County Assignment Judge Elvin R. Simmill was about to preside over the trial in the case of State of New Jersey vs. Dr. Carl Coppolino. It would receive national attention. Aware that I had helped Judge Smith with the State vs. Lynch case, he asked for my help in the event he needed legal research, which I provided during the trial. At age 30, Dr. Coppolino, an anesthesiologist at Riverview Hospital in Red Bank, New Jersey, left work on disability because of a heart condition. He supported his family with monthly benefits from a disability income insurance policy, royalties from books he had written, and the salary of his wife, Carmela, also a physician. The Coppolinos were neighbors of Lt. Colonel William E. Farber and his wife Marjorie, who was Carmela's friend. Marjorie wanted to stop smoking. Carmela suggested that Carl, an expert hypnotist, could help her. Carl hypnotized the attractive and shapely 48-year-old woman. He also took advantage of the fact that she felt drawn to him and was willing to be his "love slave." Thus began a torrid affair of which Marjorie's husband disapproved.

The affair between Carl and Marge gradually waned, and, in April 1965, the Coppolinos moved to Longboat Key, Florida. When Carmela failed the Florida medical examination, Carl, in desperate need of money, began dating a wealthy divorcee named Mary Gibson. At 6:00 a.m. on August 28, 1965, a phone call from Carl awakened Dr. Juliette Karow, the Coppolino family physician. He tearfully said he had just found his wife dead from a heart attack[1]. Dr. Karow went to the house and examined Carmela's body. Although puzzled because women in their thirties rarely suffer coronary failure, she found no evidence of foul play and signed the death certificate. Forty-one days later, Carl married Mary Gibson.

After her husband died, Marjorie Farber moved next door to the Coppolinos in Florida. Hoping to rekindle her romance with Carl, she was incensed when Carl married Mary Gibson. She visited Dr. Karow and told her that Carl murdered Carmela, saying that she had been a friend of Carmela's for many years and had not known her to have heart trouble. Dr. Karow suggested that

---

1. https://www.encyclopedia.com/medicine/diseases-and-conditions/pathology/heart-attack

Marjorie meet with Sheriff Ross Boyar. She did so, telling him that Carmela's death was suspicious. She also revealed that during a trip to Miami for a tryst, she and Carl devised a plan to kill her husband, Colonel Farber. She said Carl gave her a syringe and a deadly drug that would kill him without leaving a trace. On July 30, 1963, she tried but failed to fully inject her husband, losing her nerve at the last moment. Instead, she telephoned Carl for help. He came over, helped at first, but then smothered Colonel Farber to death with a pillow.

Sheriff Boyer sent a report to Monmouth County Sheriff Paul Kiernan, who turned it over to Monmouth County Prosecutor Vincent Keuper. Although Colonel Farber had been dead for over two and a half years, Keuper secured an order for the exhumation of his body. The authorities also exhumed Carmela Coppolino's body in Florida. Dr. Milton Helpern, chief medical examiner for the City of New York, performed autopsies of both bodies. He found evidence of succinylcholine chloride, an artificial form of curare used by anesthesiologists, in both bodies. He concluded that someone had strangled Colonel William Farber because his cricoid (part of the larynx) was fractured. These findings led to dual murder charges against Dr. Carl Coppolino in New Jersey and Florida.

Dr. Carl Coppolino, with his attorney F. Lee Bailey at the Monmouth County Courthouse in Freehold, New Jersey

MURDER, MEDIA, AND METAMORPHOSIS

ON AUGUST 9, 1966, defense attorney F. Lee Bailey, the most famous criminal defense attorney of the second half of the twentieth century, announced that he was taking Dr. Coppolino's case. Bailey first came to nationwide attention for his victory in the second murder trial of Dr. Sam Sheppard[2], a surgeon accused of murdering his wife. He later served as the attorney in several other high-profile cases. He represented Albert DeSalvo, who was the "Boston Strangler," a serial killer responsible for at least eleven women's murders in the early 1960s, and Patty Hearst, who was kidnapped in 1974 by the Symbionese Liberation Army and either under duress or willingly (accounts differ) committed severe crimes with SLA members. He defended US Army Captain Ernest Medina[3] for the My Lai Massacre[4] in Vietnam in which US forces tortured, raped, and/or killed hundreds of civilians in the village of My Lai in 1968. Bailey was also a member of the 1995 "Dream Team[5]" that successfully defended former football star O. J. Simpson[6], who was accused of murdering his former wife Nicole Brown Simpson[7] and her friend Ron Goldman[8].

Bailey's first move was to request Dr. Coppolino's release on bail. In opposition to the motion, prosecutor Keuper put Monmouth County Physician C. Malcolm Gilman on the stand to establish that there was a high probability that Coppolino would be convicted of murder and should not be released. Bailey discovered a major discrepancy during his cross examination. Marjorie Farber said that Copppolino smothered her husband to death, but Dr. Gilman opined that strangulation was the cause of death. Bailey asked him why New Jersey authorities waited eight months after learning of Mrs. Farber's allegations to exhume the Colonel's body. Dr. Gilman admitted that the delay occurred because he believed that there was not enough information to justify the

---

2. https://en.wikipedia.org/wiki/Sam_Sheppard

3. https://en.wikipedia.org/wiki/Ernest_Medina

4. https://en.wikipedia.org/wiki/My_Lai_Massacre

5. https://en.wikipedia.org/wiki/Dream_Team_(law)

6. https://en.wikipedia.org/wiki/O._J._Simpson

7. https://en.wikipedia.org/wiki/Nicole_Brown_Simpson

8. https://en.wikipedia.org/wiki/Ron_Goldman

exhumation. The implication was that even the State of New Jersey did not believe Mrs. Farber's tale for eight months!

Marjorie Farber and attorney George Chamlin

Two attorneys for Marjorie Farber, Warren M. Goodrich from Florida and West Long Branch, New Jersey attorney George Chamlin, visited Prosecutor Keuper before the trial. Their mission was to protect their client from prosecution as a conspirator in her husband's murder. They insisted she would only take the stand if she could testify that she was in a hypnotic trance at the time of her husband's death and could not act of her own free will. Keuper reluctantly agreed to this stipulation because he did not have a case without Marjorie Farber's testimony.

I watched in amazement as Bailey begin jury selection on December 5, 1966. He had memorized every known detail about the background of each prospective juror. He would break the ice by asking about the status of a potential juror's business and then inquire about the juror's family, the number of whose children he had committed to memory. His intention, he told the jury panel, was to attack Marjorie Farber's credibility and motivation. He intended to establish the fact that Marjorie Farber's husband had died of a heart attack, not murder. He would admit that Carl Coppolino was an adulterer but would prove that he was not a murderer.

Prosecutor Vincent Keuper rose to deliver his opening statement. He accused Carl Coppolino of taking William Farber's wife and life. Coppolino deserved the death penalty for breaking two commandments: "Thou shalt not covet thy neighbor's wife, nor shalt you covet thy neighbor's life." Bailey argued that no murder took place, so Coppolino was not guilty. He then launched a powerful attack on Marjorie Farber: "This woman drips with venom on the inside, and I hope before we are through, you will see it drip on the outside," he said forcefully. After a pause, he said "This woman wants this man so badly, she would sit on his lap in the electric chair while somebody pulled the switch, to make sure no one else gets him." He concluded by saying this is not a murder case at all, but rather monumental and shameful proof that hell hath no fury like a woman scorned.

The first prosecution witness was Marjorie Farber. She retold the story she had told Sheriff Boyar: that she was under Coppolino's spell ever since he had first hypnotized her to get rid of a smoking habit. She was powerless to deny him anything. He kept saying that Farber had to go. He gave her a syringe with a deadly solution and told her to inject Farber while he was sleeping. At the last moment, her nerve failed, but not before she had injected a minute amount of the fluid into Farber's leg. When he became ill, she summoned Coppolino to the house. Coppolino first administered a sedative, then attempted to suffocate Farber by wrapping a plastic bag around his head. Farber turned blue. Marjorie begged Carl to stop, which he did. Bill Farber was still alive, and when he recovered, he and Carl got into a terrible argument.

Carl left around 5 AM but returned the same morning and gave Bill another injection. Bill became groggy and told Carl to leave. The two men argued again, and Carl came out of the bedroom saying, "That bastard has got to go. He has threatened me and my family. Nobody is going to talk to me like that." Marjorie begged Coppolino to go, but he finished giving Farber the injection and said, "he is a hard one to kill. He is taking a long time to die." Coppolino then pulled the pillow out from underneath Bill's head, put it over his face, and leaned his full weight down on it. Marjorie then rose to show what Coppolino did and testified that Carl wanted to turn him over "so he'll look like he died in his sleep." He opened Farber's eye and said, "He is dead." Carl then told Marjorie to write a note to the children saying, "Please don't disturb Daddy, he is sleeping."

Marjorie concluded her direct testimony, saying that after Bill died, they went to Carl's house, where she asked him what they should do. Carl told her to call Carmela and have her come over and look at Bill. When Carmela arrived, she found Farber dead, noting that apart from being "all blue down one side," there was no outward sign of distress to the body. At Carl's urging, she signed the death certificate, citing coronary thrombosis as the cause of death.

Bailey then began his cross-examination. Marjorie testified that she neither hated nor liked Carl Coppolino. She did not call the police but covered up the death of her husband to hide the murder. While he was murdering her husband, she could not interfere because she was under hypnosis. Even though she was in a hypnotic trance, she could not kill her husband because she did not want to. She thought she was still in love with the defendant and that she was also in love with her husband. She felt sorry for Col. Farber but could do nothing to interfere with his demise because of the hypnosis. Marjorie denied being in a trance while testifying at trial. Carl lost control over her when he and Carmela moved to Florida. She also said that Carl told her not to worry about any autopsy of her husband.

Bailey then asked Marjorie about her trying to kill her husband with a poison. When Coppolino arrived at her home, she testified she was glad her husband was still alive. She got the needle under his skin by hypnotic compulsion and against her will. Although she pushed the plunger and got some fluid into him, it did not kill him. Bailey's cross examination continued,

Q. When Carl came over, did you say: Look Carl, what about this poison? I gave him a little, and it didn't kill him. Did you have a conversation about why it didn't work? Why did you smile? Is there something funny about this case?

A. I think it is very serious. I am sorry; I smiled.

Q. You won't smile again, I hope. Now, following your abortive attempt to inject the poison, your feelings toward your husband were of affection, I take it?

A. Ummm. If I were to say that I had no feelings at that particular time, that would be an honest answer.

Q. Then, the answer that you had before when you said that you were glad that he was still alive, I take it is not correct?

A. Yes, that is correct.

Q. When Carl came in at your request, treated your husband, and during this time you felt glad and not homicidal, is that right?

A. I was relieved.

Q. Were you under this hypnotic trance and at his direction and control at the time you said, 'Stop it, Carl?' Was that compulsion?

A. I would like to think the real me was coming through.

Q. That the real you was coming through. Was the real you, the homicidal you or the non-homicidal you, Mrs. Farber?

A. I am not a homicide.

Q. You never participated in any killing, did you?

A. Never.

Q. Never. This whole story is a cock-and-bull story, isn't it?

Objection! Sustained.

Bailey asked if Carl had a reason to kill William and if he talked about any threats to Marjorie when he said "Bill has got to go" the first time. She said "No." When asked if the purpose of the killing was to facilitate her intimacies with Carl, she said she did not know.

Bailey brought out that Mrs. Farber and her husband were having marital difficulties at the time of his death. She had collected $50,000 in insurance and inherited all her husband's property. He also questioned her about her teenage daughter Victoria finding her father's body and thinking he was sleeping. Majorie told her Bill was resting, and she then cooked her a hamburger. Bailey then returned to the trance. Marjorie admitted that while she was in a trance-like state, she could perform her household duties, drive an automobile, and visit friends. She did not walk any differently, like a zombie or have glassy-eyed stares. Bailey asked why she moved next to the Coppolinos in August 1965, despite wanting to avoid getting into Dr. Coppolino's trances again. Why did she not try to move away from the man who had made her a killer? Her answer was that she stayed overnight in the Coppolino house as a guest but did not then have a romantic interest in Carl.

Bailey then delved into Marjorie's relationship with Carmela. She went to see Carmela's body after she died because she "loved the girl." Asked if she loved Carmela when she was running around with her husband, Marjorie said Carl used hypnosis to force her relationship with him. She had "a normal, friendly relationship with Carm." She denied saying to Carl's mother a day or two after Carmela's death that she might be the next Mrs. Coppolino.

Bailey produced a paper dated July 30, 1 PM signed by Marjorie releasing Carl A. Coppolino, M.D. from all responsibility for the case of her husband, William Farber. The document said that "Dr. Coppolino wishes to be released because Mr. Farber refuses to be hospitalized even though he knows he may have had a coronary. Dr. Coppolino only gave emergency care."

Shifting tactics, Bailey ridiculed Farber's claim of having been an unwilling but helpless participant in the murder. He said he would produce medical testimony to prove such obeisance impossible. He hacked away, constantly reminding the jury of her adulterous and jealous behavior and, most of all, her age. "This fifty-two-year-old woman ..." was a repeated theme, as if this were reason enough to explain Farber's vitriolic accusations. Perceptibly, the mood of the courtroom swung against her. After enduring a two-day ordeal, Marjorie Farber lost her credibility.

On redirect examination, Prosecutor Keuper queried Mrs. Farber about the threats Coppolino made to her after her husband's death. Her response was that "he told me that if I ever did anything about reporting my husband's death that, first, nobody would believe me; and second, that, and even more important to me, was that he would have me declared insane and institutionalized." Keuper also asked her if Colonel Farber had a heart condition, to which she answered "no."

The other key witness for the prosecution was Dr. Milton Helpern, Chief Medical Examiner for the City of New York. He described his findings from the autopsy he performed on Colonel Farber's exhumed remains. The decedent's arteries and heart appeared normal. His examination of the Colonel's larynx disclosed a double fracture of the cricoid cartilage. He said that could only occur if there was considerable localized force pressing hard against that area. It was Dr. Helpern's opinion that death therefore resulted from the compression of the neck.

Baley asked if the rough handling of the body during disinterment caused the cricoid fracture. Dr. Helpern replied that the decedent's shirt and tie were in place and there was no sign that the exhumation caused an injury. He also said that strangulation could also cause the cricoid fracture. He did not cause the fracture during his autopsy. If someone had broken the cricoid before death, Helpern agreed that there would be evidence of hemorrhage. But, after three years, it would not be detectable anymore. He admitted that no bleeding would result if the cricoid was broken after death.

Prosecutor Keuper rested his case, and Bailey began his defense. He called Doctors Joseph Spelman and Richard Ford[9], both experienced medical examiners. They testified that the cricoid fracture occurred postmortem. They also opined that William Farber's heart showed obvious signs of advanced coronary disease sufficient to kill him. Two New York City doctors with expertise in hypnotism debunked Marjorie's trance story. Dr. Leo Wollman testified that "it is impossible to have a subject do something or perform an act which they felt they are morally unable to do." Further, a layperson would observe that someone in a trance would exhibit slow, sometimes slurred speech,

---

9. https://www.encyclopedia.com/people/literature-and-arts/american-literature-biographies/richard-ford

delayed response, and slower physical responses than ordinary. Further, there was no such thing as a continuing trance lasting over weeks or months. His opinion was that Mrs. Farber did not remain hypnotized.

Bailey then called Carl Coppolino to the stand. He admitted hypnotizing Marjorie Farber in February 1963 to help her stop smoking and one other time six or seven months later. When he went to the Farber home on July 30 in response to Marjorie's call, he made a tentative diagnosis that Farber had suffered a coronary episode. He recommended hospitalization, but Farber refused. Coppolino said he then went home and returned about 10 or 11 AM to find the Farbers arguing. He reiterated his suggestion that Bill go to the hospital. Because both refused, he asked Marjorie to sign the release, removing him from any responsibility for this case. That was the last time he saw Colonel Farber alive. He denied everything Marjorie Farber said about what transpired thereafter. He learned of Farber's death when Marjorie called Carmela that night.

On cross examination, Prosecutor Keuper asked Coppolino about his affair with Marjorie. Was she inclined toward adultery because of serious marital problems with her husband? Coppolino testified he gave her succinyl-choline chloride to use if she wanted to kill her dog. During the rest of the cross examination, Coppolino stuck to his direct testimony. He denied taking any homicidal actions resulting in Col. Farber's death. [4]

F. Lee Bailey's delivered a forty-minute summation to the jury entirely from memory. He quoted testimony and documents verbatim with no notes. He ridiculed Marjorie's story of being Coppolino's hypnotized love slave, arguing he did not have the power "to turn human beings into instruments of homicide against their will." Marjorie's "habit of slipping in and out of hypnosis" was "matched only by her convenient memory." He pointed out that to her, Carl was a gentle physician one moment and a killer the next. If Carl wanted to kill Colonel Farber, why did he not simply give him an overdose of the drugs he treated him with on July 30? Enriched by $50,000 from her husband's estate, the motive of the "hell-bent" Marjorie Farber after Carl married Mary Gibson was "to get this defendant at any price." He called her story of the strangulation an impossible one: "you cannot fracture the cricoid cartilage, or any part of the larynx that way—the chin gets in the way. He asked what sort of woman would tell her two teenage daughters about her affair and murder, and then casually make a hamburger for one of them while the Colonel remained lifeless in his bed? "I wonder if she just let him die," he concluded, "out of spite." Finally, he told the jury that he did not ask Carl if he had murdered Colonel Farber because "I wouldn't subject my client to such an indignity."

Prosecutor Vincent Keuper began his summation by saying, "I hold no brief for Marjorie Farber. Her acts, to me, were disgusting. Both must answer for the killing of Colonel Farber." Admitting that the jury might not buy her trance story, he said, "maybe I can't buy it either. But in this case, Carl Coppolino had a willing subject—Mrs. Farber." She attempted to kill her husband because Coppolino told her to. Besides, Coppolino did not deny the murder accusation. Keuper asked the jury to give considerable weight to Dr. Helpern's testimony. It should measure his reputation against the testimony of a defense witness "who has examined the evidence for five minutes." He concluded that Carl Copppolino was a man who "takes advantage of his poor wife" and induces her to sign the death certificate.

I reviewed a draft of Judge Elvin Simmill's jury charge and made some suggestions. He reviewed the vast array of conflicting medical evidence. He told the jury that to convict, it must find that Coppolino was guilty of murder "beyond a reasonable doubt." That evening, large trucks bearing the logos of the major television networks, CBS, NBC, and ABC parked across from the courthouse. They hooked up to the power lines, and floodlights lit up the Monmouth County Courthouse. TV reporters arrived in the parking lot by helicopter. After deliberating for less than five hours, the jury returned a verdict of "not guilty."

Dr. Carl Coppolino's second trial began in Naples, Florida, before Justice Lynn Silvertooth on April 3, 1967. The State of Florida charged him with the first-degree murder of his wife, Carmela Coppolino. Carmela was alive and well on August 28, 1965. The next morning, she was dead. The autopsy of her exhumed body four months later did not discover a natural cause. Toxicological investigation disclosed a puncture wound in the left buttock like that which a needle would make. The needle track suggested the injection of something into her body that might have caused her death. Carl Coppolino was an anesthesiologist and had used succinylcholine chloride in his practice. It is a muscle relaxant that, in the absence of artificial respiration, will cause a cessation of breathing. Dr. Coppolino and many others believed it would be undetectable in the body after death. Coppolino had bought a quantity of it in June. Prosecutor Frank Schaub said Carmela could not have injected herself because she was right-handed. She died instead because of the injection of this deadly drug by the defendant.

Schaub produced Dr. Milton Helpern, who testified that he performed an autopsy on the exhumed body of Carmela Coppolino. She was in good health at the time of death, and he could not determine the cause of death. He therefore gave certain portions of Carmela's body tissue to Dr. C. Joseph Umberger, a toxicologist in his office, for chemical analysis and tests. Several witnesses on both sides had testified that succinylcholine chloride was undetectable in the body. Dr. Umberger claimed he could separate certain unwanted acids from the embalming fluid and isolate the silver salt of succinic acid. However, he still had to develop a test to detect succinic acid. He described to the jury the complicated process he employed to design such a test. By using it and other novel procedures, he found succinic acid in abnormal amounts in Carmela Coppolino's brain tissue. He concluded with "reasonable scientific certainty" that Carmela's death from a toxic dose of succinylcholine chloride was "consistent" with his findings.

Schab recalled Dr. Helpern, who opined based upon Dr. Umberger's findings that Carmela died from an overdose of succinylcholine chloride. The State called two other doctors who also testified that her death resulted from a toxic dose of that substance. On cross-examination, F. Lee Bailey launched an incisive attack on the medical witnesses. He then moved to strike from the case the testimony of both Dr. Umberger and Dr. Helpern. He argued that neither doctor could give normal levels of either choline or succinic acid in the brain. They also failed to produce proof that succinic acid from a dose of succinylcholine could penetrate the blood-brain barrier. The blood-brain barrier is a defense system that prevents toxic substances in the blood from entering the brain. It supplies brain tissues with nutrients and filters harmful compounds from the brain back to the bloodstream. Bailey argued that the tests undertaken in the Umberger laboratory were not adequate to be given evidentiary status. Dr. Umberger's theories and Dr. Helpern's opinion that an injection of succinylcholine chloride was "possibly" or "probably" the cause of Carmela's death or even the "exclusive possibility" thereof, did not prove that Coppolino murdered his wife. Judge Lynn Silvertooth denied the motion.[5]

During the non-medical phase of the trial, Marjorie Farber testified about the crimes of infidelity committed by her and Carl Coppolino. Over repeated defense objections, she said that between Spring 1962 and January 1964 she and Carl, who was still married to Carmela and living in New Jersey, were "lovers." She and Carl made several trips together, including trips to Florida. She said Coppolino made incriminating statements about his wife's death in front of her. After his wife's death, she overheard Carl say on the phone, "They've started the arterial work and that won't reveal anything." Bailey had won a ruling preventing the prosecutor's use in the Florida trial of evidence from the New Jersey trial. Schaub could not show a similar pattern in the deaths of both Colonel Farber and Carmela, including that succinylcholine figured in both cases. The ruling also prevented cross-examination of Marjorie about her in-and-out hypnosis and seduction. The attempted murder of her husband was also out of bounds.

State Attorney Frank Schaub leaned heavily on the fact that Coppolino was running short of cash. He portrayed the doctor as a heartless philanderer, determined to wed Mary Gibson for her considerable fortune. Carmela Coppolino's refusal to grant Carl a divorce had scotched that idea. Instead, Coppolino began eying his wife's life insurance policy for $65,000. With that and Gibson's bank account, he was financially secure. "There's your motive," Schaub declared.

Coppolino refused to testify on his own behalf. Bailey was stunned, later calling it "a terrible mistake." On April 28, 1967, the jury found Dr. Carl Coppolino guilty of second-degree murder, a verdict that saved him from the death penalty. Judge Silvertooth gave him a life sentence at the state prison in Raiford, Florida.

F. Lee Bailey appealed Coppolino's conviction to the Florida District Court of Appeals. The Court stated that there was a lack of literature and case law to guide the trial and appellate courts about the admissibility of Dr. Umberger's novel tests. Regardless, the Court of Appeals upheld the judge's decision to admit Dr. Umberger's tests as valid evidence. [6]

In 1993 the US Supreme Court held in *Daubert v. Merrell Dow Pharmaceuticals, Inc.* that the subject of an expert's testimony must be founded upon "scientific knowledge" and meet a "standard of evidentiary reliability." The expert's opinion must be more than subjective belief or mere speculation. The trial judge must function as a "gatekeeper" of expert testimony to ensure that all scientific testimony or evidence admitted is relevant and reliable. When determining the admissibility of expert testimony, the judge must consider four factors: (1) whether the theory can be, and has been, tested; (2) whether it has been subject to peer review; (3) the known or expected rate of error; and (4) whether the theory or methodology employed is generally accepted in the relevant scientific community. [7] F. Lee Bailey was ahead of his time in the Coppolino trial. The Florida Supreme Court did not include the *Daubert* standard in its rules of evidence until 2019. If this standard had been in place during the Coppolino trial, the judge might have prevented the testimony of Doctors Umberger and Helpern, leading to a not guilty verdict.

The Florida District Court of Appeals also rejected Bailey's argument that the verdict should be overturned because second-degree murder applied only to unpremeditated murder. Deliberate use of drugs or poisons to murder bespeaks premeditation. The court ruled that because the evidence supported a first-degree murder verdict, Florida law permitted the jury to find the accused guilty of a lesser offense even if the evidence did not prove that offense.

The appellate court agreed with Bailey that the trial judge made a mistake by letting Marjorie Farber testify about the infidelity crimes committed by her and the defendant. It held, however, that the crime of adultery was not as heinous or violent as the crime of murder. Therefore, it was highly improbable that the jury would infer from such testimony that Coppolino was likely to commit murder. Considering the trial judge's error in the context of the entire record, the appellate panel concluded that the error was not harmfully prejudicial to Cooppolino. Bottom line: he got a fair trial.

Paroled in 1979 after serving 12 and 1/2 years, Dr. Carl Coppolino died on April 23, 2017, at age 85. He remains among the very few people ever charged with two entirely separate "love triangle" murders. In retrospect, a 1966 conversation between two women in Florida sparked criminal trials in two states, one ending in an acquittal, the other in a conviction. Did Dr. Carl Coppolino commit the perfect murder, or was he a victim of his ex-girlfriend's jealousy? Would a Florida have convicted him under more stringent modern requirements for the admission of expert testimony? These questions remain unanswered. The Bible may have pronounced the last judgement on Dr. Coppolino: "Be sure your sin will find you out" (Numbers 32:23), "for judgment is without mercy to the one who has shown no mercy." (James 2:13).

As my clerkship was ending, I noticed that Judge Smith's secretary and other judges' secretaries were terribly upset. They had received a new employee manual issued by newly appointed Monmouth County Administrator Theodore Narozanick. They were accustomed to flexible and lenient supervision by their judges. They now had to follow specific terms and conditions of county employment. I read the manual and was pleased to note that it entitled new Monmouth County employees one vacation day for every month worked during the first year on the job. We were leaving our posts and could not take vacation days. I therefore wrote a memo to Mr. Narozanick on behalf of the law clerks requesting eleven months of vacation pay by check since our terms were ending. After Narozanick said no, I and another law clerk visited Joseph Erwin, the Director of the Mounmouth County Board of Chosen Freeholders. We presented our case and showed him the manual. He picked up the phone and asked Narozanick, "Ted, did you write this?' Narozanick answered "yes," and Freeholder Ewin immediately shouted, "pay them!"

Mr. Narozanick reworded the employee manual to avoid any future ambiguity related to law clerks, but I won my first case. Little did I realize at the time that I would be involved in much larger causes and eventually play a key role in county and state government.

Chapter 3: Media and the Rush Hour Radicals

Transportation is the center of the world. It is the glue of our daily lives. When it goes well, we don't see it. When it goes wrong, it negatively colors our day, makes us feel angry, and curtails our possibilities. — Robin Chase

In 1966, my father cleverly introduced me to the beautiful Sandy Vaccarelli by asking me to bring a sandwich to his beauty shop while she was under a hair dryer. That was during spring break while I was still in law school. The following summer, I wanted to find someone to date. I asked my father about the girl under the dryer. He had her phone number, so I called her. She thought it was my father calling about a hair appointment. When I corrected her, she said "Oh, you are the guy who goes to Yale." I said to myself, "this is going to be difficult," but I asked her to the movies, anyway. We saw "The Sound of Music" after which I told her she looked like the signing actor Julie Andrews. That sealed the deal, and we were married a year after I graduated from law school.

Sandy's father, Dr. Lloyd Vaccarelli, was an extremely outgoing and likeable dentist in Fair Haven. His wife, Dorothy Steinman, was a Southern belle from Richmond, Virginia. Dorothy's mother and Sandy's grandmother, Berta Garton, was the daughter of James Henry Garton, who fought for the Confederacy in the Civil War. A carpenter and coffin builder by trade, he built the first coffin to hold the body of General Stonewall Jackson after friendly fire killed him. During the battle of Gettysburg, he was part of General Pickett's charge on the third day and suffered wounds. He kept himself alive by collecting rainwater with his hat and coat and keeping his wound clean.

Dorothy, a daughter of the Confederacy, did not believe in the "Lost Cause" myth that glorifies the Confederate States as fighting for a heroic cause that was not about slavery. She and Lloyd were friendly to everyone they met, including children in their neighborhood, regardless of their ethnicity, race, or background. Doc had his office in his home, and Dorothy was his receptionist. As young patients were leaving, she would offer them hard candy to make sure they would return.

Sandy and I got married in 1967, and we moved into our first house in Little Silver, New Jersey, where our daughter Kimberly Jean was born in 1971. I was then an associate in the firm of Drazin, Warshaw, Auerbach, and Rudnick in Red Bank. I did civil and criminal trial work and volunteered as an adult and juvenile public defender. In 1970, I transitioned to corporate law as in-house counsel at The Mutual Benefit Life Insurance Company in Newark, New Jersey. The Little Silver station on the North Jersey Coast Line (NJCL) was within walking distance from my house, so I commuted to work by train.

So why am I writing about trains? The history of the decline, fall, and resurrection of the North Jersey Coast Line (NJCL) is worth knowing for three reasons. First, it shows how citizens can come together and make the government address critical issues that affect their life and work. Second, it describes how local newspapers and broadcast media, now rapidly disappearing throughout the country, played a vital role by promoting public advocacy, arousing public opinion, and forcing elected representatives to make the trains run on time. Third, because transportation accounts for about a third of total US greenhouse gas emissions, passenger rail is vital for reducing US greenhouse gas emissions and combating global warming.

The Jersey Shore on the Atlantic Ocean and Monmouth Park Racetrack in Oceanport have long been popular with vacationers. The Long Branch Railroad began providing service to and from New York, Newark, and Jersey City in 1875. During the Gilded Age[1] (1870s and '80s), many notables, including Edwin Booth, Jay Gould, Frederick Douglass, and Mary Todd Lincoln frequented Long Branch. Several presidents, including Arthur, Garfield, Grant, Harrison, Hayes, McKinley, and Wilson, stayed there in the summer. Charles J. Guiteau shot President Garfield in Washington, DC on July 2, 1881. To speed his recovery, the railroad laid a spur line from the Elberon Railroad Station to the porch of Francklyn Cottage, a local residence in Long Branch. He died there two months later.

---

1. https://www.britannica.com/event/Gilded-Age

MURDER, MEDIA, AND METAMORPHOSIS

On June 30, 1882, a notable railroad accident happened on the Long Branch Railroad, with few fatalities. Five of the seven cars on the "lightning express train" that was running at a speed of forty miles an hour plunged from a trestle near Little Silver into Parker's Creek, an arm of the Shrewsbury River. Of the two hundred passengers, only three died, and one third sustained slight injuries. Former president Ulysses S. Grant pulled himself out of a smoking car window. He emerged without his hat, but with his morning cigar still between his teeth and a slight cut on the leg. Saying he was "all right," he directed the movements of rescuers.

I became one of the 10,000 riders commuting to and from work in 1970. The Pennsylvania and Jersey Central Railroads that had operated the railroad had gone bankrupt. Conrail, a freight carrier, took over and ran passenger rail service for the New Jersey Department of Transportation (DOT). Service on the rail line had become very unreliable, unsafe, and unsanitary when I joined the ranks of commuters. The former "Daily Register," former local news bureaus of the Asbury Park Press and Newark Star-Ledger, and New Jersey Monthly magazine covered these issues extensively and sparked a commuter revolt. It would be led by "rush-hour radicals" and their spouses.

———————

IN THE WINTER OF 1978, service on the NJCL was so terrible that I got together with a small group of commuters to figure out what to do. We gathered in the home of John Mortensen, a former Little Silver council member, to brainstorm. Mark Magyar, a junior reporter for the local newspaper, the Daily Register, joined us. We asked him how we could focus public attention on our plight. His advice was to become "radicals in three-piece suits" and undertake deliberate acts of civil disobedience.

"COMMUTERS SET PROTEST act; area residents stop payment on Conrail checks", Daily Register, March 1, 1978

OUR FIRST MOVE WAS to have four members of the group stop payment on the checks they used to purchase Conrail monthly commuter tickets. They gave the money to me instead to deposit in my attorney trust account. On March 6, 1978, I wrote a letter to Mr. Edward G. Jordan, the Chief Executive Officer of Conrail, informing him I was holding the ticket money. I said I would turn it over to his company as soon as Conrail provided safe, on-time rail service. The following excerpts from my letter describe why this desperate action was necessary:

> The complaints of my clients are well known and have been thoroughly publicized. Trains on the North Jersey Coast Line are dirty, unsanitary, and uncomfortable. The cars lunge and leak; they are poorly lit; and they lack heat in the winter and air conditioning in the summer. But worst of all, your trains are unsafe and consistently late. State officials have recently cited an on-time performance of 44 percent this winter, meaning that your customers

were late 56 percent of the time. The impact of this on the commuters' jobs and family life has been devastating, and it is reasonable to expect that many people will move out of the area to the detriment of the Shore economy if the situation continues to deteriorate.... The State of New Jersey is faced with a crisis in mass transportation... which affects not only my clients and all other commuters but also the general public. People from all walks of life ride the trains: senior citizens, shoppers, the blind and handicapped, bettors, the poor, and many others. Many of these people do not own automobiles, and some are physically unable to drive.... In fact, mass transit is a crucial factor in our national commitment to revitalize our cities, conserve energy and abate air pollution. Thus, the problem of the North Jersey Coast Line is of national importance. It offers us the following challenge: can the American system of free enterprise and democratic government... accomplish what has been achieved already in virtually every other industrialized country in the world: fast, safe, and efficient railroad transportation.

Other commuters sprang into action. One evening, a homebound train sped by the Middletown station without stopping. A group of Middletown commuters stood in front of the locomotive at the Red Bank station, forcing Conrail to arrange alternate transportation for them. On another occasion, Little Silver commuters tried to flag down an express train one hour after their regular train was canceled. They had to jump off the tracks when the train failed to slow down. While we were at work, three dozen disgruntled commuter wives visited the state Commuter Operating Agency in Trenton. They complained loudly that their husbands were coming home too late because of train delays. "We'll be back," they warned the terror-stricken state employees, "if train service doesn't rapidly improve."

At my suggestion, our group adopted the name "Irate Shore Commuters." Our first official act was to distribute copies of a "Commuter Manifesto" on the morning trains. It called on riders to demand better passenger rail service and catch the attention of Conrail and the government.

Service continued to deteriorate, and commuter complaints rose to such a pitch that New Jersey Governor Brendan Byrne warned the DOT and Conrail that he would "no longer tolerate foot-dragging" on efforts to improve service on the former Erie Lackawanna and New York and Long Branch lines. A week later, two high-level DOT officials, who faced heavy criticism for their handling of mass transit operations, abruptly resigned.

"Commuter Revolt: What Drives Them," Daily Register, 3/5/78.

On March 5, 1978, Doris Kulman wrote about what caused the commuter revolt in the Sunday Register. It still resonates as a succinct explanation for the angst of today's middle-class suburbanites in America:

> They are the men who did everything right. They got educations, and they got good jobs. They overpaid for a house in the suburbs to give their kids good schools, their wives, gardens, and their Collies, half-acres to romp on unleashed. They pay their taxes. Their natural habitat is the executive suite. Why, then, are these men standing in the middle of the railroad tracks, clutching their attaché cases, and daring a locomotive to run them down? Because the frustrations of commuting Conrail are more than man, or woman, can bear. Because the middle-class is tired of being dumped on. Because they are members of a privileged class, usually able to order society to meet their needs and are enraged to discover themselves powerless against an unresponsive bureaucracy. Because they are heirs to the American vigilante tradition. And because they learned from the civil rights protests, and the campus protests and the Vietnam War protests, that confrontation politics works.

"1,000 COMMUTERS LET Off Steam," Daily Register, 3/15/78.

To address rail service complaints, acting DOT Commissioner Russell H. Mullen scheduled a meeting with commuters on March 14 at Red Bank Regional High School. Over 1,000 angry riders and their wives packed the auditorium. Two new commuter protest groups joined the fray: Monmouth

County Commuter Wives and Shore Commuters for On-time Service. Members of the latter group arrived at the meeting late because of a long train delay. Speaker after speaker aired complaints about deteriorating passenger rail service. The audience shouted and jeered as elected officials and DOT representatives tried to answer their questions. Mullen promised improved communications, closer monitoring of service, and immediate service improvements.

GOVERNOR BYRNE INSTRUCTED DOT officials to speed up train repairs and locomotive rehabilitation. The State of New Jersey also purchased the rail lines operated by Conrail. These included the North Jersey Coast, Northeast Corridor, Morris and Essex, Main/Bergen, Montclair/Boonton, Raritan Valley, Atlantic City, and Pascack Lines. I sent Conrail the $400 train ticket money I was holding as a gesture of good faith, hoping for train service improvements.

Unfortunately, trains continued to be late or "annulled," a fancy word for "canceled." Two trains derailed, and one caught fire. Oblivious to these problems, the DOT proposed a rail fare increase in April 1978. At the public hearing on the fare increase, the Irate Shore Commuters alleged that Conrail employees were accepting kickbacks and disregarding union contract requirements. The company was using poor accounting procedures, overpaying for diesel fuel, and making multiple payments for the same job. Conrail allowed a mobster to take cinders from a plant without paying for them. Undaunted by these criticisms, the DOT's Commuter Operating Agency approved the fare increases.

The Irate Shore Commuters challenged the agency's decision in the Appellate Division of the New Jersey Superior Court. The money needed to file the appeal came from 2,500 commuters on the morning city-bound trains who contributed $1 each. I argued that the DOT had not supported the fare increase with the financial data required by the applicable statute. The three-judge Appellate Division panel agreed and postponed the effective date of the fare increase for three months to allow the DOT to submit supplemental data. [8]

Although we did not stop the fare increase, we won a major victory. During oral argument, DOT representatives revealed that its multi-million-dollar contract with Conrail had never been audited. Radio stations, TV news broadcasts, and local newspapers in the New York metropolitan area pounced on this news. They broadcast my argument that absent an audit, "the evil the state statute was supposed to prevent—namely, the overcharging of the commuters by Conrail, was unchecked." Concurrently, Congressman James Howard, D-NJ, blasted the DOT for failing to apply for hundreds of millions of federal mass transit funds sitting unused in Washington, DC.

The public outcry finally prompted Governor Byrne to appoint a new Transportation Commissioner named Louis J. Gambaccini. A former commuter and general manager of the New York/New Jersey Port Authority's PATH light rail system, he brought to the DOT the expertise needed to make critical decisions to clear up the mass transit mess and implement the Governor's mandate to "put it all together."

GAMBACCINI'S FIRST move was to create a new agency to replace the much-maligned Commuter Operating Agency. The Public Transportation Act of 1979 established "New Jersey Transit." Its mission was and is to operate safe, reliable, and affordable public transportation. The statute incorporated my suggestion that the agency's governing board include at least four public members. New Jersey Transit acquired ownership of the property, roadbeds, bridges, and equipment of the rail lines in the state. Unfortunately, the new agency still depended on Conrail, Amtrak, and other entities for the operation of passenger rail service. In addition, long-standing plans, and funding for the extension of electrification of the NJCL remained in limbo.

"COMMUTERS BLAST ELECTRIFICATION delay," The Daily Register, September 1, 1983

On March 6, 1978, I wrote a letter asking the State Division of Public Advocacy to investigate why the DOT was not using public money for railroad improvements and not providing good rail service for New Jersey commuters. State voters had passed a large public transportation bond issue referendum in 1968 that included $41.9 million for electrification of the North Jersey

Coast Line from South Amboy to its southern terminus at Bay Head. The purpose of this project was to eliminate a time-consuming engine change from diesel to electric locomotives at South Amboy. Only electric-powered trains could traverse the tunnels under the Hudson River to New York Pennsylvania Station. Because electric lines ended in South Amboy, diesel trains had to carry riders the rest of the way to Bay Head.

I asked what, if anything, the DOT had bought with the bond issue money? Why had DOT not spent the balance? To what extent had inflation eroded the purchasing power of the funds? Why had the DOT failed to take advantage of more than $241 million in unclaimed federal transportation funds designated for New Jersey? Had there been a breach of public trust by state officials? Were we witnessing a "Rail-gate coverup"?

Coast Line from South Amboy to its southern terminus at Bay Head. The purpose of this project was to eliminate a time-consuming engine change from diesel to electric locomotives at South Amboy. Only electric-powered trains could traverse the tunnels under the Hudson River to New York Pennsylvania Station. Because electric lines ended in South Amboy, diesel trains had to carry riders the rest of the way to Bay Head.

SOON AFTER BEING SWORN in, Gambaccini unveiled a $600 million program called "TRANSPAC" for public transit projects. It included $120 million from the NY/NJ Port Authority, which helped garner an additional $480 million of federal transit funds. At a TRANSPAC hearing, the Irate Shore Commuters, Commuter Wives, and Shore Commuters for On-time Service demanded the electrification of trains from South Amboy to the end of the line. While preparing for the hearing, I found an obscure bill passed May 14, 1974, by the New Jersey Senate directing the DOT to electrify the NJCL to Bay Head as soon as funds were available. I argued that the availability of funding under TRANSPAC would trigger this legal mandate that the NJCL be electrified. I warned Commissioner Gambaccini that he and other DOT personnel would be subject to criminal prosecution for breach of public trust and nonfeasance in office if they did not move forward with the project.

Rather than litigate, Commissioner Gambaccini presented an electrification plan for the NJCL using funds from TRANSPAC and a $475 Transportation Bond issue approved by the voters in November 1979. Phase one would extend electric lines from South Amboy to Matawan and phase two to Long Branch. It included the purchase of new locomotives and rail cars, plus repairs to tracks, bridges, signals, stations, and yards on the entire line. The commuter groups accepted this proposal.

Meanwhile, passenger rail service continued to be unreliable, unsafe, inefficient, uncoordinated, uncomfortable, and unsanitary. DOT had spent millions of dollars on capital improvements to negligible effect. Representatives of the agencies having authority over various aspects of rail operations differed sharply over the assignment of blame. At a Senate transportation committee hearing in Trenton, NJ, I pointed out that the NJCL was being "operated in whole or in part by seven or eight organizations, very few of which had commuters as their primary interest." I noted Conrail was primarily a freight railroad and Amtrak was only concerned with long-distance passenger service. Coast Guard regulations demanded that river bridges be opened whenever necessary for river traffic. "As a result," an Asbury Park Press editorial pointed out, "thousands of commuters have been forced off the rails and into automobiles and buses, aggravating the energy and pollution problems." A New York Daily News editorial noted, "The activist organizations born of the Monmouth County commuter revolt have headlined the poor operation of the commuter railroad. Now they have focused the spotlight on the tangled responsibility for running the commuter lines. The key to efficient commuter service is in the questions Monmouth County commuters have raised."

To address these issues, we asked Rep. James J. Howard, D-NJ, who represented the Monmouth County towns served by the NJCL, to start an investigation by the House Surface Transportation subcommittee of which he was a member.

"Commuter Heads to Take Fight to Capital," The Sunday Register, 8/1/80.

Congressman James J. Florio, D-NJ, chair of the House Committee on Interstate and Foreign Commerce, conducted a hearing on September 2, 1980. Congressman Howard testified that regarding responsibility for service, "commuter service is like the runt of the litter—no one wants it." An editorial in the Sunday Star Ledger, September 7, 1980, titled "No joy for riders," summarized my testimony:

> John D'Amico of Oceanport, speaking for the Irate Shore Commuters, provided a grim, caustically accurate summary of the plight of the railroad commuter: "The interests of freight shippers, boats, long haul rail passengers and the labor unions are favored over the needs of the tens of thousands of people who must struggle to get to and from work—and pay ever higher fares for the privilege."
>
> He observed that the Department of Agriculture provides more specific guidelines—and better protection—for livestock shipments than Conrail does for passengers. Livestock cannot be shipped in unheated cars in winter or in unventilated cars in summer. The North Jersey Coast Line, he emphasized, "would be illegal if it were used for livestock."
>
> Part of the problem can be traced to the original error of entrusting the management of passenger service to Conrail, a freight carrier with little sympathy for or understanding of commuter needs.
>
> A new agency ought to be created to coordinate activities and be fully responsible for providing safe, dependable service to rail commuters. The movement of lips does not move passengers.

"*AGENCY BOLSTERED ON takeover of state's commuter rail lines,*" *The Star-Ledger, March 24, 1982*

In 1981, Congressman James Florio, lost the closest gubernatorial election in New Jersy's history to Assemblyman Thomas H. Kean by less than 2,000 votes. The change to a Republican Administration meant we would lose DOT Commissioner Louis Gambaccini's leadership, which made the future of public transportation uncertain. Before his departure, Commissioner Gambaccini invited me to accompany Deputy Executive Director Martin Robins, the "brains" of NJ Transit and New Jersey's leading transportation expert, to Washington, DC to advocate reform of federal railroad laws. We met with the staff of the Senate Commerce Committee, New Jersey Senator Bill Bradley, Congressmen Howard and Florio, the US Department of Transportation, Amtrak, the US Railway Association, and the Coalition of Northeastern Governors. Our aim was to give state agencies like NJ Transit greater control over the operation and cost of passenger rail service.

Martin Robins used his thorough knowledge of archaic railway labor laws and regulations to lobby for extensive reforms. His efforts bore fruit. Congress passed the Northeast Rail Service Act of 1981, relieving Conrail of responsibility for operation of commuter rail service. I helped Robins prepare a report about commuter rail operation options, but I disagreed with its recommendation that a new regional public corporation for passenger rail operations should take over for Conrail. I argued that NJ Transit should be directly accountable to rail passengers and taxpayers and that it would also be better able to control costs and manage union contract negotiations. These factors would produce better productivity and more efficient operations. Martin and Commissioner Gambaccini agreed that a successful collaboration between five state transit agencies was unlikely and that the best course would be for New Jersey to proceed independently of its neighboring states.

NJ Transit assumed operation of New Jersey passenger rail lines in 1982. Unfortunately, the agency soon found itself in a precarious financial position because of the plan by the Administration of President Ronald Reagan to eliminate federal operating subsidies. New Jersey Congressman James Howard, chair of the House Public Works Committee, fought the good fight with but could not prevent the funding cuts. To offset operating budget deficits, NJ Transit proposed a series of fare increases and service cuts. My reaction was that these actions were idiotic and represented a return to the vicious cycle which led to the bankruptcy of the private railroads. At a rally at Newark Penn Station, I pointed out that rail service could not compete with the private automobile in terms of speed, comfort, or convenience. The only thing railroads and buses had going for them was the price. Absent that advantage, New Jersey would be on a fast track toward mass transit collapse and economic chaos.

"Fare rise may sound transit's death knell," Asbury Park Press, July 13, 1982

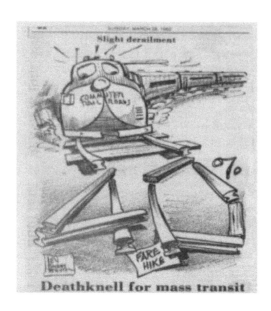

AT A HEARING OF THE joint appropriations committee of the Legislature I argued that only an adequate and dependable source of long-term funding for NJ Transit could provide the safe, fast, efficient, and reasonably priced rail and bus transportation essential to the general welfare, economic growth, and stability of the state. The legislature did not heed my advice. I therefore proposed at a fare increase hearing that NJ Transit shut down public transportation when it ran out of money. I said this would push the legislature to find a solution, quoting Samuel Johnson's famous observation: "When a man knows he is going to be hanged in a fortnight, it concentrates his mind wonderfully." [9]

Meanwhile, the DOT had spent $170 million of taxpayer money to electrify a 5.5-mile stretch of the NJCL from South Amboy to Matawan. Concurrently with electrification, NJ Transit purchased $55 million worth of new Comet II trains and seven locomotives for the NJCL On April 23, 1982, retired Judge Theodore Labrecque, chair of NJ Transit's North Jersey Advisory Committee and the Monmouth County Transportation Coordinating Committee, performed the honor of flipping on the switch inaugurating electrified rail service from New York and Newark to Matawan, New Jersey. The unanswered question was whether NJ Transit would be required to turn off the switch to commuter rail service statewide.

David Pindar, Chair of the Shore Commuters for On-Time Service, argued that the agency's capital improvements program, including electrification of the NJCL, was creating "a gold-plated railroad which no one can afford to ride." I added that the dedication of the new equipment was reminiscent of the christening of the Titanic. Newly appointed DOT Commissioner John P. Sheridan agreed. Without additional appropriations from the state, he said, "we are taking it down to the day when we will have no transit system left—no buses, no train, and no road system."

"NJ Transit may let itself go broke," The Daily Register, July 14, 1982

THE THREE COMMUTER groups, now consolidated as the Shore Commuter Coalition backed my proposal to halt commuter rail service if the Legislature did not give reliable funding, rather than relying on exorbitant fare increases. The New Jersey Transit Board agreed and voted to cancel the bus and train fare increases slated to go into effect. Governor Thomas H. Kean announced after the board's vote that he supported this action. John McGoldrick, a Harvard College and Law School classmate, and public member of the NJ Transit Board, agreed, saying that increasing fares instead of increasing ridership is "a slow pathway to disaster." Fortunately, the state government responded positively. Appropriations were increased.

To address long-term funding needs, Governor Kean renewed his proposal for a transportation gasoline tax increase. The Shore Commuter Coalition pledged its support, and the Legislature finally passed the Transportation Trust Fund Act on July 10, 1984. [10] The voters also passed an amendment to the New Jersey State Constitution to dedicate 2.5 cents of the motor fuels tax to transportation purposes. More good news came from Congressman James Howard, who persuaded the federal Urban Mass Transportation Administration to grant NJ Transit initial funding for electrification of the 16-mile stretch of the NJCL from Matawan to Long Branch.

"Morning Becomes Electric," The Daily Register

It was a long time coming, but electrified trains finally rolled into Long Branch, New Jersey, in June 1988. The NJCL Electrification and Signal Project brought in new trains and improved the railroad tracks, making mass transit on the Jersey Shore faster, safer, and more comfortable. There would be fare increases and service issues in the years that followed, but I felt that my hard work and that of my fellow agitators had paid off. A June 7, 1988, Register editorial summed it up this way:

> D'Amico, a resident of Oceanport and an insurance lawyer, was in the forefront of a strong movement to improve conditions which had deteriorated along the North Jersey Coast Line. He was the leader of the Irate Shore Commuters, who campaigned for safe, on-time service in the late 1970s and early 1980s. "For the first six or seven years that I commuted to Newark, I was as complacent as any other commuter," D'Amico said in mid-1978, shortly after becoming a commuter activist. "We kept hearing that things were going to get better, so we rolled with the punches and learned to live with the normal breakdowns. But this winter (1977) was the worst ever." Through the efforts of D'Amico and others in groups such as

the Irate Shore Commuters, Shore Commuters for On-Time Service and Commuters' Wives, things did get better.

Subsidizing Mass Transit.

Why is it so important to subsidize mass transit? New Jersey commuters bring billions of dollars home from New York and Pennsylvania each year. Maintaining dependable rail and bus transportation is a crucial advantage of living in the Garden state. It is just as critical in other states throughout the country. Here are excerpts from my *New York Times* opinion column explaining why a viable public transportation system should matter to taxpayers who do not ride buses or trains:

- Transportation accounts for about 30 percent of New Jersey's gross energy consumption, and over 40 percent of all petroleum products consumed in the state are related to travel. Significant energy savings are possible through conservation strategies in transportation.
- Federal Clean Air Act standards for carbon monoxide and ozone (not to mention reduced greenhouse gas emissions to combat global warming) cannot be met without a substantial reduction in automobile travel in the nation's metropolitan regions through improvement of the mass-transportation system.
- Highway congestion is a matter of greatest concern to private industry, mass-transportation networks being crucial lifelines of the regional economies.
- The burden of fare increases falls regressively on transit-dependent riders, including students, disabled people, the poor, and the elderly, most of whom have no access to an automobile.
- Mass transit is funded at the fare box to cover the difference between revenues and expenses, while motorists enjoy subsidies in the form of free or low-cost facilities and services, all furnished at taxpayer expense, which do not show on the auto commutation balance sheet.
- There is no urban mass-transit system in the world that does not require and receive government subsidies. In fact, all forms of transportation are subsidized, especially the automobile, for which

we exempt land from property taxes. State, county and municipal highways, roads, bridges, and traffic-control devices are built and maintained from general tax revenues, and we devote half of all police work to traffic control at public expense.

- What is needed is an equitable and balanced transportation budget to which enough money is appropriated to hold rail and bus fares at levels that encourage, rather than discourage, ridership. Such a budget should also include additional money to repair decaying roads and bridges. [11]

The work must continue. Long range rail travel is over twelve percent more energy efficient per passenger than air travel and far less polluting.[12] Thus, it is a critical component of the effort to curtail global warming. Unfortunately, Amtrak, the national railroad of the United States, suffers from the same problems that plagued the NJCL in the 1970's and 1980's. There are very few electrified routes, freight railroads delay passenger trains on their tracks, and federal and state funding is paltry compared to subsidies for automobiles and air travel. In contrast, Europe, China, and Japan recognize the importance of passenger rail transportation to the quality of life of their citizens. They provide enough operating and capital support to maintain fast and efficient passenger rail service. China has built a 26,000-mile high-speed rail network that serves a billion and a half riders annually, with plans to double such service by 2035. The United States must improve, modernize, and expand passenger rail transportation nationwide. Some movement in that direction has occurred because of President Joe Biden's Infrastructure Investment and Jobs Act, but much more must be done.

I was only one of many "rush hour radicals" who helped bring about the resurrection of the NJCL. John Mortensen, David Pindar, Arlene Stump, Betsey Barrett, Greg Bender, and Judge Theodore Labrecque all worked hard and deserve credit. We were also fortunate to have dedicated government officials to work with. Before leaving office, Commissioner Gambaccini praised the Irate Shore Commuters, Shore Commuters for On-Time Service, and Commuter Wives for becoming a powerful political force. He said "when commuter groups were in their violent stage of open revolt, and of emotionalism, they forced their government to face the problems and do something about them. Now they have become an important part of the process and a strong, visible constituency for mass transit."

I experienced firsthand the power of concerned citizens to accomplish remarkable things when united in purpose and action. I would apply this principle later when confronting major problems and issues during my terms of public service. The same power of public advocacy is available to you, your family, friends, relatives, neighbors, and fellow citizens.

Chapter 4: Another Murder

———

I behaved myself as though he had been my friend or brother.

—-Psalm 35:14.

You shall not murder. You shall not commit adultery. You shall not steal. You shall not bear false witness against your neighbor."

—-Exodus 20:13-16.

In 1978, there were two feuding Democratic factions in Oceanport, New Jersey. To no one's surprise, the mayor and all six members of the borough council were Republican. Aware of the publicity I had received as attorney for the Irate Shore Commuters, a former councilman and others asked me to be a write-in candidate for a council. I said I would run only if both factions would also support my candidacy. Their leaders agreed to do so.

I campaigned door to door by bicycle. My pitch was that we needed two-party government. To my surprise, I was the highest vote-getter, ousting the incumbent council president. Two years later, I convinced the two Democratic groups to merge and form a new organization dubbed "Oceanport Democrats." In 1981, I sought re-election with a candidate named Walter and attorney Thomas W. Cavanagh, Jr. as my running mates. Walter was a Conrail police officer, a labor leader, past president of the Oceanport Lions Club, and Vice President of Oceanport Democrats. He was also active in Oceanport Cub Scouts and Cap League baseball. Walter's wife, Anne, was also an active and involved citizen, serving as manager of the Oceanport Gardens older adults building. She was a member of the Oceanport Fire Company Ladies Auxiliary and softball coach for the Burgundy Bears. My wife Sandy and I enjoyed getting together with Walter and Anne socially and at Democratic club functions.

Tom Cavanagh and I won, and Walter lost by only 75 votes. Walter might have won had he been able to spend more time campaigning, but Anne was in the hospital with an undiagnosed illness from which she later recovered. She was madly in love with Walter, but their marriage had become troubled. Walter had met Mary on a PATH train during his morning commute in the spring of 1981. When a teenager she lived two doors down from our house and was our babysitter. She was now 20 and a Wall Street sales assistant, and he was 42, two years younger than Anne. Apparently impressed that Walter was a cop and a candidate for borough council, Mary made advances toward him. Flattered by her attention, he asked for her a date. The first time she got into his car, she suggested they go to a motel room instead of a movie. A deeply troubled young woman searching for emotional security, Mary thought she had finally found in Walter the love of her life. Thus began a torrid affair involving weekly liaisons at motel rooms. Anne kicked Walter out of their house in November 1981.

On March 20, 1982, Sandy and I met my good friend and campaign treasurer, Dr. Louis Cuccaro, and his wife Janice, at Ilvento's Restaurant in Long Branch for a St. Joseph's Day dinner. As we were leaving the restaurant, we got the shocking news that someone had murdered Anne across the way while we dined. I visited Walter at his house the next day. He hugged me and sobbed uncontrollably. His crying at Anne's wake and funeral exceeded what I had previously experienced on such occasions. Six days later, the Monmouth County Board of Freeholders offered a reward of $5,000 for information leading to the arrest and conviction of her killer.

In May 1982, Mary called the police and confessed to fatally stabbing Anne. She agreed to wear a recording device during meetings and telephone conversations with Walter. The tape recorded his admission that "we both did it." He also admitted in the recordings to buying her dark clothing and a mask as a disguise and the knife which Mary used to kill his wife. He assured her it was a perfect crime.

On September 7, 1982, Mary pleaded guilty to the murder of Anne. She said that she and Walter plotted to kill Anne so they could marry. Anne had threatened Walter that if he sued for divorce, she would expose him for using money from the Oceanport Democratic Party to pay for his motel stays with Mary. She would also disclose that he set fire to their house in Long Branch to collect $20,000 in insurance money. Walter's plan was for Mary to wait in a dark West End parking lot while he, escorting his wife to a movie, went back to his car to retrieve his keys. While Anne waited for Walter to return, Mary stepped out from behind a dumpster and stabbed her twenty-two times. When Walter returned, he found his wife on the ground and ran into Ilvento's restaurant to call for help. After the murder, Mary took Anne's purse to Atlantic City to establish an alibi—namely, that Anne was the victim of a robbery. It was there that she disposed of it and the murder weapon, a hunting knife Walter had purchased at a sporting goods store. Mary lived with Walter and his two children after the killing. It was not long, however, before Walter ended their relationship and became involved with another woman.

Walter plead not guilty and went to trial before Superior Court Judge John Ricciardi. First Assistant Prosecutor Paul F Chaiet represented the State of New Jersey. Walter's lawyer, James Addonizio, urged him to testify. His demeanor in the witness chair ranged from casual and relaxed to appearing visibly upset. He denied his former lover's charge that he conspired with her to murder his wife so they could get married. He detailed his affair with Mary from its beginnings, and he admitted he did not resist Mary's advances. She was a "flighty young girl" who contrived to meet up with him as often as possible during their daily commute. Feigning embarrassment, he said, "Quite honestly, I was 42, and she was a very young girl, and I was quite flattered by her advances toward me."

Walter traced his fateful affair with Mary to his loss in the 1981 borough election. Defeat in his third bid for council, he said, strained his marriage. "I was disinterested, and I wasn't much of a father around the house." Anne then "told me to get out of the house," he said. He checked into a YMCA in North Jersey but never slept there. Instead, he said he spent several nights sleeping in railroad cabooses. When Mary learned he was homeless, "it was like Christmas. She got excited and told me to bring my clothes. She said she couldn't have me sleeping on the railroad."

Walter admitted he lived with Mary, but under further questioning, he disputed much of her testimony. He never gave her a "pre-engagement ring," and he had little to do with her finding the Hoboken apartment that made their meetings more convenient. Shortly after moving back home, he brought his young lover to Manhattan for an abortion. Ashamed, he said the abortion was the first of two pregnancies by Walter that were aborted.

Walter had moved back with his wife after they agreed on ground rules about trying to put their marriage back together. "Those ground rules," he said, "as we worked them out, were to spend more time with the children, that Anne and I would go out more and that I would stop philandering." Shortly thereafter, Anne guessed that Mary was trying to call Walter, and she asked Walter if that was "the bitch" on the phone? Anne grabbed the telephone and called her a "tramp" and a few other choice words. Anne told Mary that she would wipe up the streets of Oceanport with her. Then Anne went silent. She looked at her husband and said, 'you had an abortion with her?" Anne was deeply religious and "that really messed her mind up," Walter recalled.

Mary had testified that she and Walter purchased the Jacket and ski mask for her to wear during the murder. He accompanied her to a store to purchase a ski jacket but said he did it only as a favor for his former lover, whom he had not seen in more than a month. She asked him to meet her after work in his car because "she had to buy a large package that would be too clumsy to take home on the PATH train." Walter said he believed the jacket was a gift for her brother.

The key witness for the state was Dr. John P Motley, a county psychiatrist, who conducted two clinical interviews with the killer. He diagnosed Mary as suffering from a "borderline personality disorder." She lacked remorse or concern for the deceased. Other symptoms included narcissism, hostility, resentment, feelings of dependency, and paranoid fantasies. This explained her tendency towards "intense and unstable interpersonal relationships." Dr. Motley concluded that "she projected the responsibility for the murder" entirely onto Walter. She was only "doing it for him," and believed the justice system should not punish her for the murder. Addonizio tried to discredit Mary based on this testimony.

Walter tried to play down the significance of his affair with Mary. He recalled growing angry once when she introduced him as her boyfriend. "I told her it was not so. I was not her boyfriend, we were friends, and we were having a relationship," he recalled telling her. Addonizio argued to the jury that Mary was a spurned and vindictive former lover. She was the sole agent in the murder of Anne after Walter ended their affair to return to his wife.

The truth was that Mary was a naïve, troubled, and vulnerable young woman, and Walter was a selfish, middle-aged man who destroyed his family for his own pleasure. Mr. Addonizio and his client could not overcome that reality and the fact that Walter had confessed to planning his wife's murder on trial tapes. The jury found Walter guilty of soliciting his former lover Mary to murder his wife; of soliciting Mary to commit an armed robbery of his wife; of conspiring with her to murder and rob his wife; and of felony murder.

Before sentencing, Mary's Wall Street employer called Monmouth County Prosecutor Alexander Lehrer. He wanted to know when he could expect her to return to work. Lehrer replied, "in about fifteen years." Judge John Ricciardi sentenced Mary to 30 years in state prison with the requirement that she serve 15 years before becoming eligible for parole. The Judge sentenced Walter to 70 years in prison with the requirement that he serve 35 years before parole eligibility. In a separate civil case, Judge Patrick McGann divested Walter of any ownership interest in the Oceanport and Long Branch houses and awarded the sale proceeds to his children.

Walter and Mary failed to heed this warning: You have heard that the ancients were told, 'You shall not commit murder' and 'Whoever commits murder shall be liable to the court.' Matthew 5:21

Chapter 5: Metamorphosis, Media, and Public Service

I know your deeds, your love and faith, your service and perseverance, and that you are now doing more than you did at first.

—-Revelation 2:19

I thank my father, John D'Amico, Sr., who was the long-time owner of John's Beauty Salon in Red Bank, New Jersey, for spurring my interest in civic responsibility. My work as a commuter advocate had brought me a tremendous sense of satisfaction. With the help of local newspapers, broadcast radio and TV, the commuter groups had largely won the battle for improved rail service. I had also gained significant name recognition, but now I wanted to continue in another sphere of public service. I therefore decided to seek the Democratic nomination for one of the two seats on the Monmouth County Board of Chosen Freeholders (now called the Board of County Commissioners). I felt that the Monmouth County governing body should have a better mix of points of view on its governing body, there being no commuters or attorneys among its members. I also firmly believed that it was important to preserve two-party government. When one party gains full and unchallenged control, there is a danger of a laxity and corruption in the discharge of public responsibilities.

To make sure there was no connection between the Shore Commuter Coalition and my political aspirations, I resigned as its chairperson. The Monmouth County Democratic Organization nominated me to run for a seat on the Monmouth County Board of Chosen Freeholders in the 1983 election. Thomas Lynch, Jr. would be my running-mate. Tom had extensive experience and a good sense of humor. He had served two terms as Freeholder in the 1970's. He and our opponent, Frank A. Self, were from Middletown, the county's largest municipality. Our other opponent was Clement V. Somers. Clem was both a Freeholder and Mayor of Oceanport, where I was still a Councilman, and he was seeking simultaneous re-election to both offices.

The landslide victory of President Ronald Reagan in 1980 had moved a lot of independent Monmouth County voters to the Republican column. Our opponents had the additional advantage of incumbency. We knew we would need to campaign vigorously and hope for some big break to be victorious. One downside for my candidacy was the fact that Tom Lynch's name would be above mine on the November ballot; therefore, our campaign bumper stickers had to read "LYNCH-D'AMICO," not the message I wanted to send to the voters.

Democrat Ray Kramer had been elected to the five-member Freeholder Board in 1982. If Tom and I joined him, the Democratic party would gain control of the Board. The turning point in the hotly contested campaign came with an October scoop. The North Jersey Coast Line Advisory Committee had helped NJ Transit create new train schedules for the upcoming electrified train service from Matawan to New York and Newark, New Jersey. I had a copy of NJ Transit's final draft, so I persuaded the Democratic Party chairperson to print a fold-out campaign brochure that included the new schedule. We handed it to commuters at the train stations in Monmouth County in October. The brochures listed the names of the legislative, county, and local candidates running for office in the towns served by each major station. It expressed our commitment to affordable, efficient public transportation and urged commuters to vote for us to support reasonably priced, safe, dependable, and comfortable public transportation.

This was a major scoop because the company hired by NJ Transit to print the official new schedules had not delivered them in time. Our campaign flyers included the only new schedules effective on October 23, 1983, that were available to the commuters. N.J. Transit had traditionally only distributed large fold-out schedules for the entire NJCL. After the election, the NJ Transit Executive Director thanked me for giving the agency the idea to print one-page schedules tailored to individual station stops, a practice which continues to this day.

MURDER, MEDIA, AND METAMORPHOSIS

"Flawed Resume Hurts Monmouth GOP Bid," The Star-Ledger, 11/10/1983

We got our second big break when Lynch's daughter Marjorie saw Frank Self's campaign literature. An engineering student at Georgia Tech, she noticed Self's claim to have graduated Phi Beta Kappa from that institution. She told her father that no one graduated with that distinction from Georgia Tech. Instead, the equivalent honor for engineering graduates was Phi Kappa Alpha. When confronted with this disparity, Self blamed his secretary for the mistake, saying she did not know one Greek letter from another, but Democratic Chairman John Fiorino learned from both organizations that there was no record of Self's receipt of either honor. The local newspapers eagerly printed our press releases about this revelation.

Self also lied about being an astronaut, a NASA employee, and an airline pilot on resumes, campaign fliers, and in person. He misrepresented himself as a decorated fighter pilot in Vietnam. He claimed he received multiple awards, including the Silver Star, two Distinguished Flying Crosses, and the Purple Heart. At Fiorino's request, Congressman James Howard asked the Air Force to check its records to see if Self had won these awards. Howard got a letter from Lt. Colonel Thomas M. Allison saying there was no record of Self being awarded the medals. At the request of the Asbury Park Press, the National Records Center in St. Louis confirmed Howard's report about Self's service medals. When newspaper reporters asked Self to show him the medals, he said the only one could find was the Air Force Medal.

Self's most damaging exaggeration surfaced during a debate at a synagogue. When asked what he did for the State of Israel, Self said he flew for the Israeli Air Force during the 1967 Arab Israeli War, and he held up a 1980 flier so stating. Self's actual involvement was to ferry jet fighter planes to Israel but he did not take part in combat. When we raised this issue, Self said he was a victim of "misrepresentations" in the campaign literature. He maintained he did not know the flyer was being distributed. David Cohen, Self's former Republican campaign manager, claimed that Self made the flier and lied to the newspapers about it.

The papers reported on the eve of the election that Cohen and other Republican leaders were calling upon Self to withdraw from the campaign. Republican Party Chairman Fred Kniesler acknowledged that the adverse publicity hurt, but he kept Self on the ticket, hoping his running mate Clement Sommers would win and perpetuate Republican control of the Freeholder Board.

At a Sunday brunch in Howell Township, NJ, late in the campaign, I gave a passionate speech attacking our other opponent, Clement Sommers, who was running simultaneously for re-election as Freeholder and mayor of Oceanport. I quoted Matthew 6:24 and criticized him for trying to serve two masters. Mayor Ed Cordts praised my enthusiastic speech but reminded me that my colleague Ray Kramer was serving simultaneously as Freeholder and mayor of Asbury Park.

In September a week after Labor Day, the Borough of Oceanport celebrated its annual Summer's End Festival at Blackberry Bay Park. Mayor Sommers rented and rode a small elephant through the fair to encourage attendees to vote Republican. The Oceanport Democrats countered by having children wear shirts labelled "Sommers' End Festival."

The election was very close, but Tom Lynch and I won. I edged Sommers out by only 1,685 votes out of 126,521 votes cast. In effect, the county Republican ticket had "Self-destructed," with Frank Self taking Clement Sommers down in his wake. In Oceanport, Sommers received more votes for Freeholder than I did. The voters in town wanted him to remain in his county office, but they opted to elect Thomas Cavanagh as their new mayor. In addition, with the victory of two council candidates, the Democrats gained control of the Borough's governing body for the first time in 63 years.

Chairperson John Fiorino observed that by revealing Self's dishonesty about his academic, military, and professional background, local newspapers in Monmouth County presented a straightforward choice for voters. He identified Self's lie about his medals as the key issue. Republicans lost control of the Board of Freeholders because they joined the scam by not distancing themselves from Self when presented proof that he did not receive the awards.

In 2022, in the absence of local news scrutiny, the voters in New York's 3rd Congressional district elected George Santos. He aligned himself with Republicans in the US House of Representatives who falsely rejected President Joe Biden's win in the 2020 election while at the same time accepting their own election outcomes. Soon after taking office, he was indicted for wire fraud, money laundering, theft of public funds, aggravated identity theft, falsifying records, access device fraud, and making false statements to Congress and the Federal Election Commission. The Republican majority in the House of Representatives defeated two attempts to expel Santos from Congress. After a monthslong investigation, however, the House Ethics Committee issued a report alleging that Santos stole money from his campaign, reported fictitious loans, deceived donors, and engaged in fraudulent business dealings. It also found that he used campaign funds to cover personal expenses, including at luxury retailers, on cosmetic procedures and on travel.

Although over one hundred Republicans voted against the third expulsion resolution, a bipartisan super majority finally removed Santos from office in November 2023. In the last days of the 1983 campaign, Chairperson Fiorino had distributed fliers to the voters with this message: "Serving the public involves public trust. While there is no need to be brilliant or an honored veteran to serve the public, honesty and integrity are essential. Without such qualities, none are qualified to hold the public's trust in office." Jennifer Rubin from *The Washington Post* has updated and amplified Fiorino's message: "When a party decides to peddle in lies and propaganda, they can expect liars and propagandists to fill their ranks. When the incentive to mislead voters is greater than any incentive to tell the truth, you wind up with a party of charlatans." [13]

County Government at Work

A Daily Register editorial described the election of Tom Lynch and me to the Board of Freeholders as a major victory for the Democratic party, giving it control of the Monmouth County government. It noted that "Lynch is a former freeholder with a fine record to his credit. D'Amico will bring with him to the freeholder board strong accomplishments as an activist for improved transportation and a deep concern for social issues."

First, let me explain county government and what a "Freeholder" is. The term "freeholder" is a feudal anachronism, having originated in medieval England to designate a white male who owned an estate or land free and clear. In colonial times, only freeholders were eligible for election to county governing bodies in New Jersey. Slaves, tenants, and women were ineligible. I often argued that the term "freeholder" was incompatible with a democratic form of government that welcomes the participation of all citizens, including those who do not own real property, are women, or are persons of diverse racial and ancestral origin. I also found during my campaign that the use of the phrase "Board of Chosen Freeholders" to describe the county governing body confused Monmouth County residents two ways. Many believed that they could not vote for a candidate for "freeholder" because they did not live in Freehold Township, Freehold Borough, or Upper Freehold Township. In addition, most county residents were unaware of the services and programs provided by the Freeholder Board.

Like other states, county government in New Jersey operates under the commission form of government in which each freeholder is responsible for specific departments and functions. Over the past two centuries, county governments in New Jersey and elsewhere have grown exponentially in importance and scope. They now oversee regional needs and problems in the areas of health, human services, and law enforcement. County governing boards fund and manage court and jail facilities, emergency management, vocational and post-secondary education, solid waste disposal, recycling, water supply, storm water and wastewater management, environmental protection, libraries, parks, planning, consumer affairs, economic development, community development, fair housing, employment, agriculture, tourism, transportation, roads, bridges, public works, and many other agencies and programs.

To keep up with modern governance, Governor Phil Murphy changed the name "Freeholder" to "County Commissioner" in New Jersey through a law signed in 2020. This was a major step toward making county government more inclusive, transparent, understood, and appreciated. In the spirit of this change,

I will use the term "County Commissioner" instead of "Freeholder" in the rest of this book.

For five years after the hotly contested 1983 election, with only a few disagreements, the Democrats and Republicans on the Board of County Commissioners took major steps to improve the quality of life in Monmouth County. Many of the problems they tackled serve as microcosmic examples of how municipalities, counties, states, and nations should address critical issues currently affecting the United States and the rest of the world. To address environmental concerns, I suggested, and the County Commissioners approved, the appointment of three new members to the Monmouth County Environmental Council and the allocation of a full-time Planning Board staffer to implement their recommendations. I called upon the Council to lead the fight to end the dumping of raw sewage, sludge, contaminated dredge materials, acids, medical waste and other pollutants into the Atlantic Ocean and bay waters off our shores. Clean Ocean Action's aggressive 20-year campaign, helped by the County Commissioners, state and federal officials, and environmental agencies, led to the cessation of ocean dumping. Under the able leadership of Cindy Zipf, Clean Ocean Action continues to be a leading regional voice to protect waterways using science, law, research, education, and citizen action.[14]

Saving Farms

At the turn of the Twentieth Century, there were almost 3,000 farms tilling over two hundred thousand acres of fertile soil in Monmouth County. By 1984, the number of farms had shrunk to 732, encompassing only 72,000 acres. According to an April 19,1984 Daily Register editorial which addressed the problem then and speaks to the same issues today,

> ... the county's farms were swallowed in the building boom that swept down from the Garden State Parkway and brought housing developments and commercial buildings where the potatoes, corn and cabbage once grew. And there is relentless pressure on farmers to sell their land for non-agricultural purposes, pressure not only from developers but from the economics of farming. The threat to

our food supply is immediate and serious, and the continuing loss of farmland has enormous implications for the availability, quality, and price of the food we eat.

The County Commissioners used state and county funds to help the Agricultural Development Board purchase development rights from farmers who wanted to preserve their farmland for themselves and future generations. The county and state also provided aid for irrigation and soil conservation projects.

Other counties and states must act urgently and adopt similar programs. According to a report by the American Farmland Trust, America could lose over eighteen million acres of farmland by 2040.[15] Continued growth of urban development and what the organization calls low-density residential development is eating away at the most productive farmland in the world. The report points out that "well-managed farmland supports wildlife and biodiversity, cleans our water, increases resilience to natural disasters like floods and fire, and helps to combat the changing climate." The organization says we will never achieve climate goals by just reducing emissions. The US and other nations need to keep farmland and actively manage it to draw down carbon from the air.

Avoiding Nuclear Catastrophe

I was a little over four years old at the beginning of the atomic age, dramatically depicted in the movie *Oppenheimer*. In grammar school, we practiced air raid drills in anticipation of nuclear war. We planned to protect ourselves by diving under our desks. Considering that our school was 25 miles in a direct line from New York City, the likelihood was that a nuclear bomb dropped on the city would obliterate us. In our high school and college years, my friends and I agonized about the prospect of the nuclear Armageddon of World War III. Woody Allen summed up our psychological paralysis in his "Speech to the Graduates": "More than any other time in history, humankind faces a crossroads. One path leads to despair and utter hopelessness. The other, to total extinction. Let us pray that we have the wisdom to choose correctly." [16]

During my first term as a County Commissioner during the height of the Cold War, I thought about doing something about the issue. One evening at dinner, I asked my daughter Kimberly what issue was most important to her. She said she was terrified by the possibility of total annihilation in a nuclear war. That comment prompted me to draft a resolution approved by the County Commissioners and many Monmouth County municipalities in 1985. Nuclear concerns still trouble the world today as Iran seeks to develop a nuclear weapon, Russia threatens use of nuclear weapons in its invasion of Ukraine, and an increasingly antagonistic China expands its nuclear arsenal. The resolution included these main points:

- No public issue is more difficult or important than the avoidance of nuclear war, because nuclear weapons can cause damage on such a catastrophic scale as to wipe out a large part of civilization and trigger major and irreversible ecological and genetic changes whose limits cannot be predicted.
- More nuclear weapons with greater destructive potential are being added daily to the tens of thousands already deployed and more nations are seeking to become nuclear powers, increasing the risks of war resulting from accident, miscalculation or the actions of nations or groups not controlled by the superpowers.
- The arms race is extremely costly and is consuming resources that would otherwise be available for the health, safety, and public benefit of both the United States and other nations of the world.

The Resolution called for substantial, simultaneous reductions in the nuclear weapon arsenals of the superpowers. It sought to halt the proliferation of nuclear weapons and enhance their command and control. These remain essential objectives for governments throughout the world. In his farewell address to the Association of Los Alamos Scientists in November 1945, J. Robert Oppenheimer said that "atomic weapons are a peril which affects everyone in the world... I think that in order to handle this common problem, there must be a complete sense of community responsibility." We need to come together to pressure governments to decrease the number of nuclear weapons and manage nuclear risks.

The strengthening of command and control over nuclear weapons is extremely important in the New York metropolitan area. Earle Naval Ammunition Depot is in Colts Neck, New Jersey, an upscale community of horse farms, fruit orchards and country estates. The Navy transports conventional and nuclear munitions back and forth between the storage area there and a 2.9-mile pier located fourteen miles away in Leonardo, New Jersey. In Sandy Hook Bay, the Navy pier overlooks New York Harbor. Woody Allen summed up the potential for disaster in the New York metropolitan area in his "Speech to the Graduates": "what of the H-bomb? Have you ever seen what happens when one of those things falls off a desk accidentally?" According to the General Accounting Office, if a warhead is damaged, it could release a cloud of plutonium dust shaped like a cigar. This cloud could travel up to twenty-eight miles and potentially affect New York City and most of Monmouth County. The Navy responded to my concerns by installing improved traffic controls on county roads, but there are still unanswered questions. How do we know when an accident takes place? How are emergency personnel supposed to react? How will the public know what to do?

Commissioner Ray Kramer's loss to Republican candidate Theodore Narozanick in 1985 marked the end of Democratic control on the Board of County Commissioners. On January 2,1986, the Republican majority named Harry Larrison as Director of the Board in place of Tom Lynch. Ray Kramer was a "mensch," friendly, intelligent, and kind. He had served Monmouth County with distinction as County Commissioner and Director of the Board of County Commissioners from 1975 to 1981 and as Deputy Director in 1984 and 1985. He was also an Asbury Park council member and mayor from 1969 to 1985. He owned several Jersey Shore restaurants during his working career. When a server at one of his restaurants gave birth out of wedlock to future actor Jack Nicholson, Ray gave her financial support. Ray died in 1992. Five years later, Jack Nicholson won an academy award for Actor in a Leading Role in the movie "As Good as it Gets." He dedicated his Oscar to a few entertainers and others, including Ray Kramer, saying "They're not here anymore, but they're in my heart."

CURTAILING HOMELESSNESS

The fact that Commissioner Tom Lynch and I were now in the minority meant that we needed to persuade the new majority to address the problem of homelessness. A nun and other community activists approached me for advice on how to convince the County Commissioners to act. I encouraged them to keep coming to the public meetings, attract media attention, and apply pressure on the Board to produce a solution. They followed my advice, and the Commissioners approved a contract with a non-profit agency to operate a 42-bed homeless shelter at Fort Monmouth, NJ. At my suggestion, the agency agreed to provide services, such as counseling and 24-hour supervision, to the homeless people in the shelter. In a letter published by The Register on August 15, 1986, the nun and other activists wrote that "At a time when many office-holders seem not to care about the needs of middle- and low-income people, heeding only the rich who contribute large sums of money to their campaigns, John D'Amico's light shines in the darkness as one who cares about all of us and about the quality of our lives, whether we are rich or poor, black or white, male or female."

More elected officials need to care because there are about 653,104 homeless persons in the United States, and the problem is getting worse.[17] The principal cause is lack of access to housing, but poverty, mental illness, addiction, and other issues are contributing factors. Existing homes are in limited supply, and rents are rising with inflation. The result: more people priced out and ending up homeless. People experiencing homelessness face major health challenges. They have limited access to health care and are vulnerable to malnutrition, violence, and stress. They live in unsanitary living conditions and are exposed to severe weather. Homelessness is connected to declines in physical and mental health. Homeless people are at a greater risk of HIV infection, alcohol and drug abuse, mental illness, tuberculosis, and other conditions. Some cities criminalize homelessness and associated actions like sleeping in public or begging. [18]

Cities, counties, and states should increase the supply of housing affordable to extremely low-income renters and reduce homelessness by implementing land use and zoning policies, such as:

◇ Eliminating exclusionary zoning codes restricting multi-family use, such as single-family zoning.

◇ Legalizing accessory dwelling units (ADUs) and basement/cellar units.

◇ Removing or reducing minimum lot-size requirements.

◇ Revising minimum building size and floor area ratio requirements.

◇ Eliminating or reducing parking requirements for new residential construction projects.

◇ Permitting manufactured housing.

◇ Simplifying the housing permitting and development process.

◇ Creating financial and developmental incentives promoting affordable housing.

◈ Removing barriers to mixed-use residential and commercial development.[19]

In addition, cities, counties, and states should link temporary housing with remedial services, as Monmouth County does. A New Jersey law worthy of consideration permits mental health professionals to assist people in emergency shelters, either part-time or full-time, in a restricted area of the shelter.[20]

Combatting Racism

Joseph Mattice, the defense attorney in the Lynch murder trial discussed in Chapter 2, was mayor of the Jersey Shore City of Asbury Park in 1970 when a riot, including incidents of racial violence, devastated the city. Mattice embarrassed himself and his office during an interview on national television. When reporters asked him what he was planning to do to quell the riot, he said, "if we keep them on the other side of the tracks, we will be OK." Asbury Park began a slow recovery in the 1980's after Freehold native Bruce Springsteen drew attention to the city with his songs and gigs at the Stone Pony. After decades of decay and disinvestment, Asbury Park has experienced a renaissance. New construction has filled vacant lots. Small investors have renovated much of the surviving stock of stately old houses, hotels, and storefronts. A vibrant downtown features upscale restaurants and establishments. Crowds once again visit the beaches and boardwalk on the Atlantic Ocean along Ocean Avenue. The grit has faded but is not completely gone. Across the train tracks, in the neighborhoods away from the beach, poverty persists and there remains an acute need for affordable housing. Racism persists in the city, the County of Monmouth, the State of New Jersey, and the United States of America.

In 1986, I found myself in the center of a strange and ugly episode of racism. It related to the Monmouth County Board of Social Services, the county's welfare agency, to which the County Commissioners appointed me. During a closed session, the Social Services Board, with no prior notice, explanation, or documentation, voted six to three to request the resignation of the agency's long-serving Executive Director, Louis Armour, the highest-ranking African American official in the county. The resolution was based on vague charges, insinuations about deficient performance, and suggestions of mishandled funds. There was no credible evidence supporting these allegations. I therefore joined with two other conscientious board members, Maurice Scully, and Gertrude Harris, to oppose the resolution.

I argued that there was not a convincing case for Armour's dismissal, that his actions had not been ruled illegal, and that "plain and simple," he was not being treated with the respect and dignity he deserved. An accounting firm had suggested improvements to county social services. Armour and his staff therefore presented a plan to the board with responsible solutions and implementation procedures. The Board of Social Services sent the plan to its personnel committee. Instead of considering its recommendations, a majority of the board members sought Armour's resignation. They also involved the Monmouth County Prosecutor's Office.

I released a statement to the press asking, "how can Mr. Armour be faulted for refusal to implement policies when this board has not decided what those policies should be and has not provided direction?" Employees "should be disciplined only when rules have been violated," but "to punish a man who has spent a lifetime in public service before any rules have been established or broken is unfair and irrational."

Armour refused to resign, saying, "There's still a job to be done. There are still poor and homeless families out there. It's not an easy agency to administer because of the extent and variety of our social service program." The county's African American community reacted with anger. Members of its civic organizations turned out in force at the Social Service Board's public meetings, charging racism and challenging the board's actions at every turn. The NAACP and the Afro-American Society wrote letters to the members of the Board of County Commissioners seeking an investigation of the Board's request for Armour's resignation. They presented petitions containing approximately 1,700 signatures to the Commissioners urging them to put pressure on the Board of Social Services to reverse its decision.

I notified the board's Chairwoman Phyllis Marx that I would move to rescind the request for Armour's resignation. I informed her that Monmouth County

Prosecutor John Kaye had resolved the issue behind the resignation request. He found no wrongdoing in the $17,000 cash advance to Family and Children's Services, which Armour had approved, and the agency had repaid to Social Services. Members of the public shouted their support for Armour. They constantly interrupted the board's June meeting. They called board members liars and witches and threatened them for their actions against the embattled director. The board agreed to delay its vote on whether to fire Armour to study the charges its personnel committee had compiled against him.

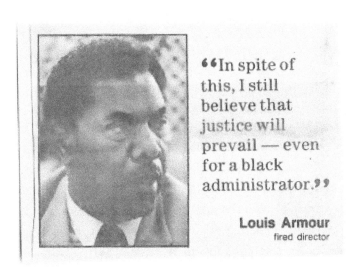

"In spite of this, I still believe that justice will prevail — even for a black administrator."

Louis Armour
fired director

AT THE SOCIAL SERVICES Board's July meeting, Armour delivered a 43-page response, rebutting the charges leveled against him. He also produced a letter from Audrey Harris, director of the New Jersey Division of Public Welfare, stating that Armour has run an effective organization, has an enthusiastic approach to administrative efficiency, and has performed his duties and responsibilities well. I proposed that the board work with Armour on administrative issues, suggested referral of the fiscal issues raised by the management audit to the board's new fiscal officer, and urged the board to develop bylaws and specific guidelines for its executive officers.

The County Commissioners had just appointed Commissioner Ted Narozanick to the board. He sided with me, but the Board voted five to four to fire Armour immediately and without pay. Armour charged the Board with racism, saying he would appeal his dismissal to the NJ Civil Service Commission. He also threatened to file a civil suit against the Board. In mid-July, however, a board member who had voted for Armour's dismissal resigned and another changed sides. The Board therefore approved my motion authorizing the Board's attorney to negotiate a settlement with Armour's attorney.

Two weeks after firing Armour, the Board of Social Services reinstated him as director with back pay. Over the vehement objection of Board chair Phyllis Marx, who was the prime mover of the attempt to dismiss Armour, the Board adopted bylaws based on state regulations that listed the duties of officers and subcommittees. It also reformed the procedures for electing officers. Mrs. Marx resigned in January 1987.

A July 30, 1986, *Daily Register* editorial said that I deserved credit "for standing tall from the outset." Though Armour won reinstatement, this unfortunate episode did a lot of damage. It tarnished the agency's image in the community and undermined its credibility. The Board of County Commissioners responded by creating a new Department of Human Services encompassing the Division of Mental Health, Division of Alcohol Services, Division of Drug Abuse Services, and the welfare Division of Human Services.

The history of the Armour affair remains relevant in the 21st century. Racial discrimination persists in various sectors of modern US society, including the criminal justice[1] system, business[2], the economy[3], housing[4], health care[5], the media[6], and politics[7]. The number of hate groups in America is at a historic high—the legacy of a long history of racism, white supremacy, and white

---

1. https://en.wikipedia.org/wiki/Racism_in_the_United_States#Criminal_justice_system

2. https://en.wikipedia.org/wiki/Racism_in_the_United_States#Business

3. https://en.wikipedia.org/wiki/Economic_discrimination

4. https://en.wikipedia.org/wiki/Racism_in_the_United_States#Housing_and_land

5. https://en.wikipedia.org/wiki/Racism_in_the_United_States#Health

6. https://en.wikipedia.org/wiki/Racism_in_the_United_States#Media

7. https://en.wikipedia.org/wiki/Racism_in_the_United_States#Politics

nationalism.[21] Elected officials at all levels of government must "stand tall" against these evils. They need to support policies that ensure equal treatment for everyone, regardless of race, ethnicity, or nationality.

As the 1986 election approached, my colleague and friend Tom Lynch revealed he had cancer and could not run for re-election. Regrettably, he would pass away on March 12, 1987. My new running mate would be a handsome young former football player, John Villapiano, then a member of the Ocean Township governing body. He brought with him a whole new group of supporters, including his famous brother, Phil Villapiano, former All-Pro linebacker for the Super Bowl-winning Oakland Raiders coached by John Madden. Our campaign manager was Chaz Uliano, an extremely able and well-regarded West Long Branch, NJ, attorney.

The Register and the Asbury Park Press endorsed John Villapiano and me for election to the Board of County Commissioners, noting that we had the edge in service. The Asbury Park Press said that I had been "a leader on environmental and transportation issues." The Register also endorsed my re-election:

> "Democratic incumbent John D'Amico, Jr. has proven to be an extremely thoughtful freeholder during the three years he has served on the board.... An attorney, D'Amico first came to politics as a commuter advocate and then was elected to the Oceanport council. The... freeholder strongly believes that, with rapid development, the county should acquire open space to protect potable water resources and provide green areas for future generations.... D'Amico is the most knowledgeable and consistent and has demonstrated an ability to think critically and act independently. Because of his contributions thus far, he definitely should be re-elected."

The New Jersey Environmental Voters Alliance, comprising leaders from environmental groups such as the Sierra Club and Clean Ocean Action, endorsed me for my leadership in the fight for a clean and safe environment. The Sierra Club's endorsement was noteworthy because I was the first county official in the country so honored. The Environmental Voters Alliance also endorsed Congressman James Howard, Chair of the powerful House Public Works Committee, who led our ticket to victory. A major highlight of our campaign was an endorsement of our campaign during a visit to Monmouth County by Senator and future President Joseph Biden.

ON ELECTION NIGHT, I eked out another close win over my opponent by 2,383 votes out of 116,630 votes cast. With this victory and that of my running mate John Villapiano, Democrats kept two out of the five seats on the Board of County Commissioners. The voters also elected our running mate, Patricia Bennett, as Monmouth County Surrogate.

Preserving Open Space

In 1986, the County Commissioners approved a $30 million bond issue to buy land for county parks. In 1987, Monmouth became the first county in New Jersey to win public approval of an Open Space Trust Fund. Property owners would contribute two cents annually for every $100 of assessed property value to meet open space and recreation needs. At my suggestion, James Truncer, Executive Director of the Monmouth County Park System, used the money to implement a "Greenbelt" strategy. Its goal is to preserve lands next to streams and tributaries flowing into the county's rivers and reservoirs. All twenty-one counties in New Jersey have followed Monmouth County's lead and established Open Space Trust Funds.

Preserving open space is a significant step county government can take toward the solution to a global problem. Fishing, farming, and mining restrictions currently protect just seventeen percent of the planet's land and eight percent of its oceans. On December 19, 2022, 190 countries approved a sweeping United Nations agreement to protect thirty percent of the planet's land and oceans by 2030. It aims to prevent the loss of biodiversity, which endangers food and water supplies and countless plant and animal species. [22]

The topography of the United States comprises a variety of ecosystems, including tundra, prairies, wetlands, forests, and deserts. It is home to tens of thousands of native species. The United States protects about thirteen percent of its land, and President Joe Biden has promised to attain the goal of "thirty percent by 2030." Biden's America the Beautiful plan relies on state governments, local groups, and Indigenous communities to conserve and restore land. It encourages the creation of new parks and wildlife corridors and offers incentives to do so. To inform decision-making, the plan pushes for more research into areas that have prominent levels of biodiversity. It also expands the definition of "protected areas" to include sustainably managed farms, ranches, and areas for hunting. All counties, states, and countries must preserve protected areas.[23]

GARBAGE

Confronted with the prospect of running out of landfill space for the disposal of garbage, in the 1980's, the Republican led Board of County Commissioners hired engineers to explore the construction of a garbage incinerator in Tinton Falls. The engineering firm they chose stood to benefit from an eventual contract. It therefore invited county officials to an all-expenses paid tour of solid waste disposal facilities in Delaware, Florida, and Europe. None of the European technologies were fully functional. The incinerators visited in the

United States produced prodigious amounts of toxic dust covering every nook and cranny of the plants.

I therefore asked the engineers for an environmental and health assessment. It said the proposed incinerator would emit multiple pollutants into the air, including sulphur dioxide, hydrogen chloride, carbon monoxide, nitrogen oxides, and sulfuric acid. Emissions dangerous to human health would include beryllium, mercury, arsenic, cadmium, chromium, nickel, and other toxins. Commissioner John Villapiano and I opposed the Republican Commissioners' bond issue for building an incinerator at the Reclamation Center in Tinton Falls, New Jersey, due to health and safety concerns. Because four votes were needed for the bond issue to fund the project, it was blocked. Meanwhile, to economize the use of dwindling landfill space, the Reclamation Center began using a process the tour group observed near Rome, Italy. Workers sorted metals and plastics from a waste stream conveyor belt by hand for recycling.

After years of delay and fierce local opposition, the County Commissioners held a public referendum on the "burning question." The voters rejected the proposed incinerator in a lopsided vote, and Monmouth County saved $250 million. In 1994, the US Supreme Court invalidated state laws such as the one in New Jersey that forced counties to handle their own solid waste within their borders. Counties could cart solid waste to any state in the country.[24] Incinerators built in other counties became white elephants.

Counties and municipalities throughout the nation continue to struggle with solid waste disposal. According to a study by Columbia University, Americans trash seven pounds of material per person every single day. That is 2,555 pounds of material per American every year. Ninety per cent of all raw materials extracted in the US are dumped into landfills or burned in incinerators. This one-way system of destructive extraction, consumption, and disposal is polluting the air, contaminating drinking water, choking the oceans, and wasting natural resources.[25]

Recycling is not working in the United States. Municipalities and counties truck residential and commercial recyclables to recycling plants for processing. The plants clean and sort them in batches, and compress them into bales of similar plastics, paper, aluminum, or glass. The centers sell the recyclables on the open market to buyers who will process them and turn them into new products. Processing and creating saleable recycled goods costs money. As with any product, profitability requires selling for a higher price than it costs to make.

Because recyclables picked up by solid waste haulers are mixed and often contaminated, batches are harder to process into new products. The most common contaminants include medical waste, plastic bags and packaging, food waste, shredded paper, scrap metal, liquids in containers, ceramics, drinking glasses, light bulbs, frozen food boxes, and other plastic-coated paper products. Contaminated recyclables fetch a lower price on the market or do not sell at all. Currently, US recyclables are no longer profitable,[8] and no one wants to buy them. On January 1, 2018, China enforced a ban on most scrap material imports because of elevated levels of these contaminants in shipments. A weak market for recyclables has forced waste-management companies around the country to go back to cities and municipalities with two choices: pay a lot more to get rid of them or dump them. Most are choosing the latter. [26] Government must enact strong laws and programs to advance recycling; individuals and corporations must recycle better, cleaner, and smarter; and we must produce less solid waste if we are to prevent the planet from being buried in garbage.[27]

Legislative Campaigns

In 1987, I was a candidate for the New Jersey Assembly along with Joseph Quinn on a ticket headed by State Senator Frank Pallone, who was seeking re-election. United States Senator Bill Bradley endorsed us, urging voters to elect the Pallone, D'Amico, Quinn slate "PDQ: Pretty Darn Quick." In between campaign stops, we approached a basketball court where a few young boys were shooting hoops. Bradley asked for the ball. With determination, the former New York Knicks forward made some impressive jump shots, leaving everyone in awe.

The Register endorsed my candidacy, noting that I had already "led a distinguished career as a county freeholder." The Register cited my support for

---

8. https://www.ecowatch.com/plastic-recycling-triangle-myth-2648460721.html

a ban on sales of non-biodegradable plastics. Even now, their spread is polluting the world's oceans, bays, and rivers, particularly when they break down into microplastics. The Register concluded that "we believe coastal Monmouth needs a representative with D'Amico's vigor and imagination. D'Amico is a candidate of intelligence and foresight. He has served the Board of Freeholders thoughtfully and, we believe, will make an excellent assemblyman."

Frank Pallone won re-election to the Senate; however, though bruised, our Assembly opponents prevailed. Assemblyman Anthony Villane resigned to take a position as state Director of Community Affairs. Confident that his political power was intact, the GOP ran Villane's son Thomas in a special election to finish his unexpired term. County Commissioner John Villapiano surprised everyone by winning the Assembly seat.

Although I lost my election bid for the Assembly, a funeral, and a series of other events in 1988 would land me in the New Jersey State Senate. The funeral followed the sudden death of Congressman James J. Howard on March 25, 1988. In a County Commissioner resolution expressing the sympathy of all county residents presented to his wife Marlene Howard, I commented that "Combining a love of people, boundless energy, a keen intelligence and consummate political skills, Jim Howard became one of the best congresspeople in the United States. His legacy includes new highways, bridges, rail lines and stations, and other major public works in Monmouth County and throughout the country. More significantly, he leaves us an example of public service at its best."

Frank Pallone won the 3rd Congressional District seat in November 1988 by defeating former state senator Joseph Azzolina. With his election to Congress, Pallone automatically surrendered the 11th District senate seat he had held for five years. In the same election, the voters overwhelmingly approved a change in the ground rules for filling vacancies in the state Legislature. The new law abolished special elections. Instead, county committee members of the political party that occupied the vacant seat in the district would select a legislative replacement to serve until the next general election. On December 10, 1988, a unanimous voice vote of eighty-six Democratic District 11 delegates sent me to the New Jersey State Senate. In an editorial titled *"D'Amico moves up. Pallone's successor has excellent credentials,"* the Asbury Park Press commented: "John D'Amico, Jr. was the logical choice of the Monmouth County Democratic Organization to fill the State Senate seat vacated by Rep. Frank Pallone, Jr.... D'Amico is well-qualified for the...office.... He's a strong advocate for extending rail service to western Monmouth County and promises to give environmental causes top priority."

SENATE PRESIDENT JOHN Russo swore me into the Senate on December 19, 1988, while my mother Elvira watched, and my wife Sandy and daughter Kimberly held the bible. I thanked God, my family, and my supporters for making this honor possible, but I made one horrible mistake. I forgot to mention that December 19 was also my wife's birthday. She deserved better, as she has been the love of my life and my best friend and supporter throughout our marriage.

Environmental Victories

During my Senate tenure in 1988 and 1989, I sponsored or co-sponsored several bills to address environmental issues. They included a $300 million open space preservation bond bill earmarking $220 million for Green Acres. $50 million funded farmland preservation, and $20 million paid for development rights for unspoiled land. I also sponsored a $50 million bond issue, creating a Combined Sewer Overflow Abatement Fund. Its purpose was to rebuild sewer systems that mix stormwater and sewage to prevent overflows during heavy rains and pollution of coastal waters with raw sewage. The voters approved both measures.

Interstate Tax Wars

Sen. John D'Amico (D-Monmouth) displays a teabag—thousands of which have been sent to New York lawmakers in protest of that state's new policy on taxing commuters—and a Dwight Gooden-signature baseball, symbolic of the senator's call for New Jersey to play 'hardball' with cross-state taxes

ASSEMBLYMAN ROBERT Menendez and I teamed up to propose a law that would bring back the Emergency Transportation Tax on non-resident commuters. To strike back against New York's taxes on New Jersey residents, our bill would tax New Yorkers working in New Jersey on their total household income. Playing "hardball" with these bills forced New York to adopt more favorable tax code provisions. The tea bag that I held in my left hand during the tax battle with New York would signal the end of my political career. It would also symbolize a major setback in efforts to prevent the attempted murder of planet Earth.

The COVID-19 epidemic sparked a new tax war in the early 2020's. New York and other states adopted a "convenience of the employer" rule. It treats days worked from home for an employee's convenience and not because of a mandate by an employer in another state, as days worked at the employer's office for tax purposes. New Jersey and other states have retaliated by creating a "convenience of the employer" test for residents of other states that impose a similar test. New Jersey also gives tax credits to its residents who work from home for companies based in other states. These measures have gained in importance as more employees work from home at least two to three days per week.

Assault Weapons Ban

I ran in the November 1989 election to keep my 11th District Senate seat. My opponent was the popular and affable Assemblyman Joseph Palaia, who had defeated me in my 1987 campaign for the Assembly. One major issue in the campaign was my vote to ban military semi-automatic assault weapons like AR-15s and AK-47s. I argued these weapons are designed to kill people and are dangerous. Palaia took the side of the National Rifle Association (NRA) and opposed the ban.

A year after I left the Senate, the Legislature passed and Governor James Florio signed a statute criminalizing the possession of over fifty semiautomatic rifles and shotguns and those with either a pistol grip, folding stock, or a magazine holding over six rounds. In 1996, the state Attorney General's Office classified guns as assault weapons if they had features like a grenade launcher, flash suppressor, bayonet mount, or telescoping stock. Unlawful possession of an assault firearm is a second-degree crime, punishable by a sentence of between five and ten years in New Jersey State Prison. [28] Unlawful possession of an assault firearm is subject to the stringent sentencing guidelines of New Jersey's Graves Act[9]. That law requires a minimum prison term for crimes committed with firearms, with a mandatory period of parole ineligibility. [29] New Jersey's assault weapons ban has been highly effective, and its statutes are models for regulation in other states.

Congress enacted a national assault weapon ban in 1994. The "Federal Assault Weapons Ban" prohibited the manufacture of certain semi-automatic firearms and large capacity ammunition magazines for civilian use. The 10-year ban,

---

9. https://www.newjerseygunlawyers.com/?page_id=28

which was signed into law by President Bill Clinton[10], expired on September 13, 2004, under its sunset provision[11]. It decreased deaths and injuries caused by mass shootings as those crimes involve assault weapons more often. [30]

An editorial published by the *Washington Post* on March 28, 2023, notes that ten of the seventeen deadliest mass killings in the United States since 2012 involved AR-15s. The names of the towns and cities where these tragedies took place have become familiar: Newtown, San Bernardino, Las Vegas, Parkland, Uvalde, and Nashville. About one in twenty US adults own at least one AR-15. Sixteen million people are storing twenty million guns designed to mow down enemies on the battlefield with brutal efficiency. The editorial concludes that "the Second Amendment does not require standing by while 6-year-olds are torn to shreds. The nation needs to act on guns. The AR-15 and weapons like it are a good place to start."[31] The proposal floated by some Republican members of Congress to make the AR-15 the "National Gun" is not.

In 1989, Brad Lawrence and Steve DeMicco (no relation), the consultants for my campaign to hold on to my State Senate seat, introduced me to the voters with this narrative:

10. https://en.wikipedia.org/wiki/Bill_Clinton

11. https://en.wikipedia.org/wiki/Sunset_provision

It's a story we all know well.

His father came over from Italy at 17. He had $6 in his pocket.

Giovanni D'Amico worked hard and started a family. John was the first born.

There was always one constant. His father taught him that serving people was an honor. He would say "You have an obligation to help others."

His mother made sure the school work got done. John was the first in his family to go to college. He graduated with honors from Harvard and then law school.

At Harvard he worked on the campaign of President John Kennedy. It was the start of his involvement with public service.

After law school John got married and started raising his own family. But he took time out to volunteer as a Public Defender to help people in trouble.

> *"I know what's right because my parents made sure of it."*

After that John led fights to improve shore commuter service. Preserve open space and safe drinking water. He even was involved with helping the homeless before others saw the magnitude of the problem.

Now John D'Amico is taking on some of the biggest fights of his life. The odds never bother John. Because you don't do things because they're easy. You do them because they're right. It was true when his parents taught him; it's true today.

John D'Amico. Senator.

The courage to make the tough choices.

John's father taught him . . . "You have an obligation to help others."

BRAD AND STEVE PRODUCED outstanding mailings:

- "John D'Amico took on the railroads, the bus lines, and the state bureaucracy. And for once, the commuters won."
- "The chemical companies and developers want to weaken environmental safeguards. John D'Amico says NO. Joe Palaia says OK."
- "Talk won't clean up our environment. The difference between John D'Amico and Joe Palaia boils down to this: John D'Amico takes tough stands. Joe Palaia just talks."

The NJ Environmental Federation, a state-wide activist environmental organization comprising forty-five civic, labor, and environmental member organizations, endorsed me. Its news release stated: "John D'Amico has been a leader in the fight to end ocean sludge dumping, he has sponsored the Green

Acres Bond Act to preserve open space, and ... he has led the successful fight to pass the Clean Water Enforcement Act (CWEA) in the Senate." Effective in 1990, the CWEA requires the Department of Environmental Protection to inspect permitted facilities and municipal treatment works annually. The law requires additional inspections when the permittee is a significant non-complier. The CWEA assesses mandatory minimum penalties for serious violations of the Water Pollution Control Act. [32]

The Clean Water Enforcement Campaign and the Sierra Club Committee on Political Education also acknowledged my support for the Green Acres bond issue and preservation and restoration of coastal and natural resources. Joan Denzer, Chair of the Sierra Club, New Jersey Chapter, said, "both issues address the critical need for purchase and preservation of the rapidly dwindling open space in New Jersey, a major priority of the Sierra Club in this state." She added, "I would like to add that I have had the privilege of working with you personally on several issues and have been impressed by your real and long-term dedication to environmental concerns."

The NJ State AFL-CIO, Communications Workers of America, political arm of the NJ State Nurses Association, the Operating Engineers Local 825, Alliance for Progress, Political Action Committee of NJ Citizen Action, Women's Political Caucus, NJ Tenants Association, and NJ Education Association also endorsed me. I began my campaign twenty-six points behind Joe Palaia, but our issue mailings and these endorsements brought me to the threshold of victory. My running mates John Villapiano and Dan Jacobson were elected to the N.J. Assembly. Unfortunately, my Senate campaign fell short by just 1,417 votes out of 56,431 votes cast. Thus, I became the first senator in NJ history to serve after not being elected to the Senate and to leave after not winning an election to the Senate.

My departure from the Senate ended a time-consuming decade of public service. Balancing work responsibilities like meetings, government functions, constituent services, and campaigning left little time for my family. I apologized to my wife for my absence. She accepted my apology. When I apologized to my daughter Kimberly Jean, she said she enjoyed working on my campaigns and eating the food at political functions. She also thanked me for the few occasions when I helped her with her school assignments. An exceptionally good student at Shore Regional High School in West Long Branch, New Jersey, she won the Presidential Academic Fitness Award in 1989. Also, Congressman Frank Pallone and Congressman James Howard's widow, Marlene Howard, presented her with the Silver Congressional Award for meeting goals in public service, personal development, initiative, and physical fitness.

After ten years of public service, I returned to the private sector and faced a career crisis. Fortunately, the good will, friendships, and associations I had gained over a decade in elective office would facilitate my return to public service, where I could resume efforts to help people and improve social outcomes in new, meaningful ways.

Chapter 6: Career Metamorphosis

———

Your word is a lamp to my feet and a light to my path.

—-Psalm 119:105.

Do not be anxious about anything, but in every situation, by prayer and petition, with thanksgiving, present your requests to God. And the peace of God, which transcends all understanding, will guard your hearts and your minds....

—-Philippians 4:6-7

In Biology, the word *metamorphosis* signifies the process[1] by which immature forms of insects[2], frogs[3], etc., develop[4] into the adult[5] form[6]s. It is "a change of the form or nature of a thing or person into a completely different one, by natural or supernatural means."[33] After my departure from public service in 1989, I would experience a metamorphosis. It would involve abrupt and challenging career changes affecting the people with whom I worked and others in significant ways.

In the 1989 gubernatorial election in New Jersey, I supported Congressman James Florio's candidacy and served on his campaign advisory committees on environmental and transportation issues. After his swearing-in, he implemented two of my recommendations. First, he forbade the burning of trash to prevent the release of harmful substances and started a recycling program for the entire state. Second, he collaborated with Senator Frank

---

1. https://dictionary.cambridge.org/us/dictionary/english/process

2. https://dictionary.cambridge.org/us/dictionary/english/insect

3. https://dictionary.cambridge.org/us/dictionary/english/frog

4. https://dictionary.cambridge.org/us/dictionary/english/develop

5. https://dictionary.cambridge.org/us/dictionary/english/adult

6. https://dictionary.cambridge.org/us/dictionary/english/form

Lautenberg to build a train station in Secaucus, NJ, named after the Senator. Commuters in northern New Jersey would no longer have to ride to Hoboken to take ferries into Manhattan. Instead, passengers change trains to Northeast Corridor trains bound for New York Pennsylvania Station.

There were discussions about me joining Governor Florio's cabinet or working in executive transportation roles after he won. None of these appointments materialized.

Largest Life Insurance Company Failure in US History

The Mutual Benefit Life Insurance Company had its origin in Newark in 1845, and its policyholders owned it as a mutual insurance company. After the Civil War, claims agents rode on horseback to find widows and pay them life insurance proceeds. The company became successful during the late 1800s and early 1900s by focusing on life insurance for the wealthy. The Great Depression of the 1930s forced the company to reduce wages, but it kept all its employees. The cafeteria in its home office building in Newark provided for many workers their only daily meal.

When I joined Mutual Benefit Life in 1970, it was the 18th largest life insurance company in the United States with assets of more than $12 billion. Over the next two decades, I received several promotions and rose to the position of Second Vice President and Counsel. I managed life and health insurance claims, litigation, and compliance with state regulations for the company.

In 1973, inflation more than doubled to 8.8%.and it would rise to 14% by 1980. Insurance companies therefore invested heavily in real estate for higher returns. Unfortunately, Mutual Benefit lost money on investments in luxury condominium developments at Fisher Island and Williams Island near Miami. The company chased profits by becoming both a major lender to and joint venture owner of speculative projects. It took risks by investing in companies outside customary life insurance investment portfolios through leveraged buyouts. The company hired inexperienced and undependable partners for these ventures and did not dismiss them for poor performance. Other wrongdoings included keeping two sets of books and giving $6.25 million in bonuses to senior managers despite knowing the company was in trouble.

Reluctant to cut their losses when they should have, some companies aggravated their problems by throwing good money after bad, but they survived. Mutual Benefit Life, the worst practitioner of this ill-fated tactic, did not. Insurance company rating agencies lowered Mutual Benefit Life's credit rating in 1991 because of its loan portfolio. This led to a rush by owners of big life insurance policies to withdraw their money. When policy surrenders neared $1 billion, Mutual Benefit executives asked New Jersey Insurance Commissioner Samuel Fortunato for state protection. He responded by placing the company under state supervised rehabilitation.

During the summer and fall of 1991, I collected information from attorneys in the company's Law Division who had experience with real estate investments and other ventures to determine the cause of the company's decline. Because he knew me from Governor Florio's campaign, Commissioner Fortunato agreed to meet with me at his home. I shared my findings with him. I also gave him a legal memorandum stating that under New Jersey law, directors owe corporations the duties of care, loyalty, disclosure, and good faith. The memo argued that Mutual Benefit's directors had violated these duties by omission. They had failed to question the speculative proposals presented by company officers. In the absence of satisfactory answers, they also failed to hire attorneys to investigate and discover critical facts as required by law. Commissioner Fortunato complained of his difficulty getting board meeting minutes. He shook his head in disbelief when I told him that the board did not create or keep minutes of their meetings.

The New Jersey Attorney General sued the senior officers and directors of Mutual Benefit Life after a 20-month investigation. The defendants included prominent members of the state and national business community. Among them were current or former heads of American Express, Public Service Enterprise Group, Automatic Data Processing Inc., Blue Cross and Blue Shield of NJ, Merck & Co. Inc., Bristol-Myers Squibb Co., and F.A.O. Schwartz. Also named was the chancellor of the University of North Carolina at Chapel Hill.

The complaint alleged that Mutual Benefit's outside directors breached their fiduciary duty to protect the interest of policyholders. They "failed to keep informed of the company's business affairs, investments, and financial condition, and abdicated their responsibility for overall management of the company" to a few insiders. The complaint also accused the company's former accounting firm, Ernst and Young, of failing to perform its duty as auditor. It certified financial statements that were materially false and hid the true state of Mutual Benefit's finances. The parties settled the case in 1999. The director's errors and omissions insurance carrier paid the State of New Jersey its policy limit of $20 million, and Ernst and Young paid $19 million. Commissioner Fortunato allocated $18 million to policyholder groups and $17 million to groups of creditors.

There should be no legal safe-haven protection for so-called "dummy, figurehead, or accommodation" directors like those who sat on the Mutual Benefit Board. This issue resurfaced in 2023. Voting-device manufacturer Dominion Voting Machines[7] sued Fox Corp. for libel. It claimed that Fox and its hosts/executives harmed its reputation by spreading baseless allegations of voter fraud as the cause of Joe Biden's victory over Donald Trump in the 2020 election. Rupert Murdoch, the board chair of Fox News, testified in a deposition that he allowed Fox hosts to propagate the falsehood that the 2020 election was stolen, even though he knew the accusations were baseless. The parties settled this case for $787.5 million. A separate shareholder lawsuit against Fox Corp., the parent company of Fox News, alleges financial harm because the board did not stop hosts from making false claims about the 2020 election.

Several cities, counties, and states are suing fossil fuel companies, including Chevron, BP, ExxonMobil, and ConocoPhillips, for climate change damages. The suits allege they spent decades actively denying the global impact of burning fossil fuels in pursuit of profits. The overall volume of climate litigation has increased exponentially both in the U.S. and across the globe with various approaches and in a larger number of economic sectors. Oil and gas companies

---

7. https://news.bloomberglaw.com/us-law-week/fox-loses-preliminary-ruling-in-voting-machine-defamation-case

are subjects of the largest number of suits. The strategic and financial impact of climate litigation on companies could be significant in terms of direct and indirect costs, with a potential adverse impact on the competitive position and financial risk profiles of some companies.[34]

My former colleagues and friends Frank Casciano, Brian Frikert, and Chip Weiss, prudently managed the ten-year process of liquidation of Mutual Benefit Life. Its real estate holdings recovered enough value to make policyholders, creditors, and employees mostly whole. I left Mutual Benefit Life in 1991 and for about a year was "of counsel" on insurance issues at the firm of Shea and Gould in New York City. Like many attorneys, however, I had harbored thoughts throughout my career about becoming a judge. In 1986, Peter J. Wallison, a college and law school classmate, served as counsel to President Ronald Reagan. The President accepted Peter's suggestion that he appoint Antonin Scalia as a Supreme Court Justice. I wrote him a letter stating that, while pleased to learn of his involvement in this selection, I was disappointed that he overlooked me. If he was looking for an Italian American Harvard Law School graduate from New Jersey, why didn't he think of me first? He replied on White House stationery that I should not be upset by the President's selection of Justice Scalia because only Italian American Harvard Law graduates from New Jersey with nine children were eligible.

Return to the Monmouth County Courthouse

While I was working at Shea and Gould, conflicts arose between managing partners, the firm dissolved, and I had to find a new job. Fortunately, I had unused credits from my work for Governor Florio. He nominated me as a Judge of the Superior Court of New Jersey. Since I was a former senator exempt from senatorial courtesy, the Senate quickly confirmed my appointment. I was sworn in on February 21, 1992. During the ceremony, my daughter Kimberly, who was a music major at Providence College, gave a thrilling a Capella rendition of the Star-Spangled Banner. I thanked my wife Sandy for her support over the years and received with thanks a robe and bible from my in-laws, Dr. Lloyd, and Dorothy Vaccarelli. I also paid tribute to my mother Elvira D'Amico and my late father John Sr., saying that "they have loved me and supported me and taught me that the heart is stronger than the intellect." I also quoted from Psalm 90:

> "The days of our lives are seventy years; and if by reason of strength they are eighty years, yet their boast is only labor and sorrow; for it is soon cut off, and we fly away... So teach us to number our days, that we may gain a heart of wisdom."

The Assignment Judge of Monmouth County assigned me to the Family Division, where I had to decide cases involving divorce, domestic violence, child abuse and neglect, child custody and visitation, alimony, child support, equitable distribution, and termination of parental rights. Nothing in my prior work or experience had equipped me to handle such matters. Then, as now, fifty percent of all marriages ended in divorce or separation. I learned firsthand that the most common causes are arguments over finances and infidelity. Less common reasons are lack of shared interests and incompatibility between partners. Whatever the cause, the impact of divorce on children was and is devastating. They feel scared and traumatized because the family they knew no longer exists, and the stability provided by intact parenthood is gone.

These issues emerged starkly in a six-month trial over which I presided. The husband had made millions trading corporate bonds. His technique was to dress and pose as a xerox technician and gain entrance to the bond trading floor of a major trading company during lunch time. He took advantage of "inefficiencies" in bond trading by comparing the price of a particular bond at different trading desks. He made a large bond purchase at the lower priced desk and sold the position at the higher priced desk. Unfortunately, when bond trading became computerized, the inefficiencies disappeared. The family income declined, and the wife could no longer maintain her wealthy standard of living. Their arguments boiled over into public displays of expletive-filled harangues in front of friends, at an outing with the husband's business associates, and in the presence of their only child, a teenage daughter. The wife filed for divorce.

I awarded generous fees to the lawyers at the trial's beginning and advised the parties to settle so that the family's net worth would not decrease further.

They did not take my advice. At the end of the case and after the payment of attorney fees, little money and few assets remained for alimony, child support, and equitable distribution. This outcome illustrated the sad reality that only very wealthy families can afford the high expense of a divorce trial.

The most critical remaining issue in the case was custody and visitation of the daughter. The controlling legal standard was and is the "best interests of the child." To help me make my ruling, I appointed attorney Susan Scarola to represent the daughter as *guardian ad litem*. She arranged for a psychological evaluation of the child and presented the report to me, the attorneys, and the parties. It recommended that the parents not fight in their daughter's presence or burden her with their adult issues—good advice for everyone. As suggested by the psychologist, I awarded the parents joint custody with a balanced visitation schedule. They did not follow the psychologist's advice or parent cooperatively; hence, the worst possible outcome: psychological destruction of their child.

This case and others that I handled reflected research documenting that parental divorce/separation is associated with an increased risk for child and adolescent adjustment problems, including academic difficulties (lower grades and school dropout), disruptive behaviors (conduct and substance abuse problems), and depressed mood. Offspring of divorced/separated parents are also more likely to engage in risky sexual behavior, live in poverty, and experience their own family instability. And as in the case I just described, children and adult offspring of separated parents are overrepresented in the mental health system. [35]

Talking to children about a divorce is difficult but essential. The American Academy of Child and Adolescent Psychiatry has suggestions to help children cope with the stress of divorce:[36]

◈ Do not keep it a secret or wait until the last minute.

◈ Tell your child together with your spouse if possible.

97

◈ Keep things simple and straight-forward and do not share more information than your child is asking for.

◈ Tell them the divorce is not their fault.

◈ Admit that this will be sad and upsetting for everyone.

◈ Reassure your child that you both still love them and will always be their parents.

◈ Do not discuss each other's faults or problems with the child.

The best outcomes for children occur when divorced parents stop fighting after the judge has signed the divorce decree. They should confine any further arguments between them to texts and emails rather than asking their children to convey them or disclose them under cross-examination upon return from a visit with the ex. Successful co-parenting requires negotiation, respect, and support. Effective co-parents support one another's actions and decisions. They make and stick to agreements about how to raise their children and do not undermine each other.

Equal sharing of parenting tasks is not necessary for successful co-parenting. Rather, parents in harmonious and effective co-parenting view each other as equally valuable and accept that they cannot control how their former partner behaves. They should work hard to recognize the value that each parent brings to their relationship with the child in terms of different skill sets, diverse backgrounds and life circumstances that can enrich their child's life. There are many resources available to help parents in this process, such as books, support groups, therapy, education, mediation, and coordination.[37]

Unfortunately, cooperation is not possible in every case. It is particularly challenging to achieve in cases where unmarried parents, without lawyers, come to court to dispute child custody, visitation, and child support. Domestic violence is prevalent between these parties and many divorcing couples. Common offenses include assault, terroristic threats, criminal mischief, criminal restraint, sexual assault, stalking, and harassment. Sometimes, the New

Jersey Child Protection and Permanency agency would remove children from their residences and place them under protective guardianship. Tragically, domestic violence sometimes leads to the homicide of former wives and girlfriends.

The Book of Revelation lists disease as one of the four horsemen of the apocalypse. The list in the Book of Ezekiel includes pestilence or plague. In modern society, these terrors are ruining the lives of countless family members, especially teenagers. Many will suffer or die from substance abuse and addiction, while others will suffer from gonorrhea, genital warts, or other sexually transmitted diseases. The media and entertainment industry's glamorization of sex, along with the abandonment of traditional values, has led to these outcomes.

America is experiencing sped up movement towards single-parent households. Particularly troubling is the decline of economic prospects for young, poorly educated male workers. Of course, there are many successful single-parent families. A case in point is my son-in-law Michael Dwyer, who worked full time while raising four wonderful step-grandchildren—Matthew, Luke, Sarah, and Rachel— before he married my daughter Kim. Dysfunctional single-parent families experience higher rates of illegitimate births, teen suicides, and violent crime. Experts advise that the most effective way to address these harmful effects is by keeping families together and supporting them in developing stability, personal responsibility, and strong work habits.

Considering all these circumstances, I desperately needed help to decide properly the cases that came before me. That help came from my wonderful wife, Sandy. Although we had been regular churchgoers during our marriage, I had never really developed the strong faith needed for this moment. I needed a spiritual metamorphosis, and Sandy proposed the solution. She was a member of a women's Bible Study Fellowship International group, and she suggested I join a men's group that had formed in our area. BSF International believes people discover their true purpose and identity by knowing God through His Word. It offers free, in-depth Bible studies in community for people of all ages around the world. Countless men and women have found peace, comfort, hope, security, and answers to life's big questions as they uncover the truth of God's Word together. [38]

My studies with BSF helped me discover powerful ancient advice to many people coming to the Family court for resolution of their troubles:

> I say then: Walk in the Spirit, and you shall not fulfill the lust of the flesh. For the flesh lusts against the Spirit, and the Spirit against the flesh; and these are contrary to one another, so that you do not do the things that you wish.... Now the works of the flesh are evident, which are: adultery, fornication, uncleanness, lewdness, idolatry, sorcery, hatred, contentions, jealousies, outbursts of wrath, selfish ambitions, dissensions, heresies, envy, murders, drunkenness, revelries, and the like; of which I tell you beforehand, just as I also told *you* in time past, that those who practice such things will not inherit the kingdom of God. But the fruit of the Spirit is love, joy, peace, long suffering, kindness, goodness, faithfulness, gentleness, self-control. Against such, there is no law. And those who are Christ's have crucified the flesh with its passions and desires. If we live in the Spirit, let us also walk in the Spirit. Galatians 5:16-25

When confronted with the reality of having to make tough decisions, I now had a powerful ally, the Lord my God. I invoked His aid through prayer as part of my decision-making process. I will not discuss others that came before me, except to say that the limited feedback I got from litigants who appeared before me after I left the Family Division, was positive. During my tenure, I tried to assist the attorneys and judges handling family court matters by writing two articles. One of them was "Bankruptcy for the Matrimonial Practitioner." [39]

The second article addressed the process of establishing alimony and child support, which was difficult and frustrating for me and other family court judges for a variety of reasons. There is often not enough money to go around. One or more parties are likely to be unemployed, or "making money under the table," and the accuracy of their estimates of expenses is usually questionable. I therefore discussed a wealth of government data available online to help courts and lawyers measure awards of alimony and child support. These include consumer expenditure surveys of the federal Bureau of Labor Statistics (included in *The Statistical Abstract of the United States*), occupational employment wage surveys published by state Departments of Labor, Monthly Fair Market Rents compiled and published by the US Department of Housing and Urban Development, and automobile insurance rates compiled by state Departments of Insurance. [40]

Speeding Justice

After three and a half years in the Family Division, Assignment Judge Lawrence Lawson assigned me to the Civil Division. My principal mission there was to settle and try civil cases. I wrote several published decisions and settled or tried a variety of personal injury, medical malpractice, and environmental contamination cases. I was troubled by a significant issue in the US trial process. Many cases that cannot be settled face lengthy trials the expenses of which outweigh any potential recovery.

N J Superior Court Assignment Judge Samuel DeSimone used "Summary Jury Trials," involving a jury hearing evidence and issuing a non-binding verdict used to help both sides settle. Summary jury trials were time-consuming, and although they helped settle some cases, they fell into disuse. I believed there had to be a better way. I invoked God's help. His answer awakened me in the middle of the night at 3 AM: "Carefully read the Court Rules of Procedure and Evidence and look for shortcuts."

I opened the rule books and read Rule 102 of the Rules of Evidence and Rule 1:1-2 (a) of the Rules of Procedure. They said that litigants may eliminate "unjustifiable expense and delay" by agreeing to relax and simplify the rules of evidence. I therefore drafted a model Consent Order for Expedited Jury Trial that parties to civil lawsuits could use to get a speedy trial and save money. The consent order limits the number of live witnesses, usually only the plaintiff and the defendant. It reduces the size of the jury to six with no alternates and the number of peremptory challenges to three on each side. Opening statements cannot exceed fifteen minutes or summations, 30 minutes. The parties can agree that the court's judgment will not go beyond a maximum limit, often the policy limit, or fall below a minimum limit, usually the settlement offer rejected by the plaintiff.

The parties stipulate to (1) the authenticity of documents, writings, and photographs; (2) the admission of business records, expert reports, and written statements of persons not giving live testimony; and (3) the reasonableness and necessity of charges in bills and invoices for services, treatments, therapies, prescriptions, goods, materials, and supplies. The judge handles objections to documents in a preliminary hearing, redacting inadmissible material and admitting the exhibits into evidence so that the attorneys can give them to the jurors when they deliberate. The judge and counsel determine which parts of depositions and interrogatories they will present to the jury, as well as how they will explain matters beyond the jury's expertise, such as medical matters. The attorneys may use definitions of medical terms and procedures from medical dictionaries, diagrams and charts from medical textbooks, and anatomical models. These materials help juries understand injuries like herniated discs and open-and-closed reduction of fractures.

Attorneys may only object to misstatement of the evidence or improper arguments. As a result, the average length of an Expedited Jury trial is only one to one and one-half days from preliminary hearing to jury verdict. The benefits are significant: happy litigants, engaged jurors, saved expert testimony fees, eliminated scheduling issues, and saved time and money. Expedited Jury Trials produce legally binding jury verdicts without the travail of lengthy trials. I therefore recommend their use as an alternative dispute resolution option for litigants, bench, and bar.

Lauded at its birth by the Asbury Park Press for "speeding the wheels of justice," the trial bar and major insurance carriers have accepted the Expedited Jury Trial procedure. The New Jersey Administrative Office of the Courts has implemented it statewide. Expedited Jury Trials are frequently used in New Jersey courts to quickly and inexpensively resolve civil cases that cannot be settled. Other states, including California, Florida, Arizona, Colorado, Nevada, New York, Oregon, South Carolina, and Utah have enacted Statutes providing for Expedited Trials patterned after the New Jersey procedure. Other states whose Rules of Procedure and Evidence are like the Federal rules, as are

New Jersey's, have established expedited civil jury trial programs by rule. In these states a consent order like the New Jersey form can implement expedited jury trials. [41] Other state courts should consider the procedure.

New Jersey's judiciary has an excellent reputation throughout the nation. In thirty-eight states, appellate and trial judges get voted in, either in an initial election or a "retention" election following a first term. Supreme Court justices face competitive elections in twenty-two states. In only eight states, including New Jersey, are judges appointed rather than elected. They are not subject to the adverse influences attendant to fundraising and the quest for votes. More states should follow the New Jersey example, where the Governor appoints all judges and the state Senate confirms the appointments after extensive background checks and hearings before the Senate Judiciary Committee. If reappointed after serving an initial term of seven years, judges have lifetime tenure until age 70.

The US Supreme Court's popularity has decreased because Justices Alito and Thomas, along with Thomas' wife Ginny, did not disclose expensive trips, gifts, favors, and land purchases. There is also a growing concern that the high court is deciding cases based on politics, rather than law. The Supreme Court has tried to restore its reputation for impartiality by adopting a code of ethics. Legal experts consider it to be weak. It contains a lot of "should not's" and very few "musts." It also lacks any enforcement process.

The US Supreme Court and other states should adopt a strict Code of Judicial Conduct like the one promulgated by the New Jersey Supreme Court. It prohibits NJ judges from engaging in any political activity or attending any political functions. They must always act in a manner that promotes public confidence in the independence, integrity, and impartiality of the judiciary; avoid impropriety and the appearance of impropriety; and disqualify themselves in proceedings in which someone might question their impartiality or the appearance of their impartiality. Judges may not receive any active income from any source other than their salaries while they are on the bench. Neither a judge nor a member of the judge's family living in the same household can accept a gift, bequest, favor, or loan from anyone except a gift of nominal value incident to a public testimonial; books supplied by publishers complimentarily for official use; or an invitation to the judge to attend a bar-related function or activity devoted to the improvement of the law, the legal system, or the administration of justice. [42] The NJ Supreme Court can order the temporary suspension of a judge and has the statutory authority to remove a judge for misconduct. Judges who face charges before their initial seven-year term may not be reappointed even if exonerated of any ethical violations. A judge may also be barred from future judicial service, even after the judge leaves the bench.

During my tenure as a Judge of the Superior Court, my former running mates Tom Cavanagh and Joseph Quinn joined me on the bench. Another judicial colleague was Paul Chaiet, the prosecutor in Walter and Mary's murder trial. For rest and recreation, a group of judges would play golf on the weekends. Most of us, including me, were poor golfers, but we shared the belief that golf will be a great game when perfected. Two judges, however, were excellent players. One of them, Judge Ira Kreizman, originated a golf contest called the "Vicinage Cup" in which judges from various counties competed. The Monmouth County team prevailed on a couple of occasions based on the play of Ira and my good friend, Judge Benn Micheletti.

In his younger days Benn was a "scratch golfer" (averaging par over eighteen holes and maintaining a zero handicap) and was a catcher on minor league baseball teams. He was the "Renaissance man" of the group. He sang opera in college, following in the footsteps of both of his parents, who sang at the Metropolitan Opera in New York, a place I frequented as an opera lover. He taught business law at the Massachusetts Institute of Technology (M.I.T). As a corporate attorney who had majored in chemistry at N.Y.U., he persuaded the CEO of the manufacturer he worked for as a corporate attorney to sell off its asbestos division before asbestos was banned as a carcinogen.

Another regular member of our golf foursome was Judge Alexander Lehrer, who was the Monmouth County Prosecutor at the time of Walter and Mary's trial. "Hollywood Al" was brilliant and flamboyant. If he agreed with your cause, he would be your strongest advocate. When he was in grammar school, he was riding on a school bus with the two sons of convicted and executed Communist spies, Julius, and Ethel Rosenberg. When the other kids on the bus discovered who they were, they harassed them. Al immediately came to their defense and protected them from physical harm. Judge Lehrer's demeanor on the bench was volatile. As the Family Division's Presiding Judge, he would alternate between compassion and rage to intimidate litigants into settling their cases.

The last member of our foursome enjoyed statewide reputation as the best judge for settling cases. Brilliant, funny, and empathetic, attorneys called Judge Robert Feldman "Lehrer without the scare." While sitting in the Family Division, one of his assignments was enforcement of child support. Monmouth County Sheriff's officers would round up men with significant child support arrears. They would bring them to court in groups of four linked with handcuffs called the "chain gang." New Jersey courts no longer follow this barbaric practice. Judge Feldman conducted a brief hearing with one of these defendants, whose name I have forgotten. I will call him Alex Jones in dishonor of the far-right radio show host, who repeatedly claimed that the 2012 Sandy Hook Elementary school shooting was a hoax. He owes millions of dollars of compensatory and punitive damages to the families who lost their children in the massacre.

Judge Feldman: Mr. Jones, I see you owe $20,000 in back child support. How much can you pay to reduce the balance?

Jones: I don't have to pay.

Judge Feldman: Why?

Jones: Because I am Jesus Christ.

Judge Feldman: Mr. Christ, have you read your book?

Jones, hesitantly: Well, yeah.

Judge Feldman: Do you remember the part that says, "give to Caesar what belongs to Caesar, and give to God what belongs to God."?

Jones, hesitantly: Well, yeah.

Judge Feldman: You can call me Julius, and if you don't make a payment, I will throw you into my dungeon.

I retired from my judgeship in 2002. My good friend and boss, Lawrence Lawson, the first African American Assignment Judge in New Jersey, thanked me for being a dependable, loyal, and supportive jurist. He said I had been an "innovative" judge, citing my invention of the Expedited Jury Trial. Larry and I enjoyed a wonderful evening together with our families in 2016 when the *New Jersey Law Journal* bestowed on us its "Lifetime Achievement Award."

Soon after retirement, my good friend Donald Lomurro invited me to join his law firm. I did so because of Don's reputation as an outstanding lawyer and excellent businessperson. My practice area was Alternate Dispute Resolution, including arbitration and mediation. The work was interesting and the interaction with my colleagues and outside attorneys was enjoyable. Little did I realize I would soon return to public service.

MURDER, MEDIA, AND METAMORPHOSIS

Chapter 7: Metamorphosis of and by Parole

———

Is this not the fast that I have chosen: To loose the bonds of wickedness, To undo the heavy burdens, To let the oppressed go free... And that you bring to your house the poor who are cast out; ... Then your light shall break forth like the morning, Your healing shall spring forth speedily, And your righteousness shall go before you....

—-Isaiah 58:6-8

People do not usually talk about "parole," except when a well-known criminal like Sirhan Sirhan, who assassinated Senator Robert Kennedy, becomes eligible for parole consideration. So why should you care how well parole works in your state? The answer is that it is a vital component of the criminal justice system. *Parole* is a French word meaning "word." "Parole" in the criminal justice context is a period of supervised release during which a prison inmate may serve the last portion of his or her sentence outside the gates of prison. The parolee gives his or her "word of honor" or promise to follow certain terms and conditions and not commit another crime.

In a well-functioning parole system, the decision to parole a prison inmate is based on an expectation that he or she will not re-offend. Of course, it is impossible to predict with 100% accuracy what every parolee will do. Under New Jersey's Parole Act, once the punitive aspect of a sentence (one third) has been served, an inmate has a constitutionally protected right to be considered for parole and is presumed to have a legitimate expectation of release on his or her parole eligibility date. Nonviolent adult inmates are eligible for administrative parole. The inmate must finish rehab and follow prison rules to be paroled. A hearing officer or parole board panel will deny parole upon a finding that "there is a reasonable expectation that the inmate will violate conditions of parole." [43]

Parole standards aim to motivate prisoners to follow the rules and participate in programs while in jail. The anticipation of parole helps maintain order and security in prisons. It also motivates inmates to become law-abiding citizens after release. Parole systems also save taxpayer money. For example, the New Jersey Department of Corrections (DOC) budget was approximately $1 billion per year in 2019, costing the state $33,000 per year or $90 per day to house an inmate. The cost of parole supervision was only $7,000 per year per parolee, or $19 per day. Even adding the expense of in-patient substance abuse treatment, the total cost of parole was still half the cost of incarceration. Ex-prisoners who succeed on parole gain employment and become taxpayers rather than welfare recipients.

When parolees succeed, there is less crime. There are fewer victims suffering physical and mental health-related injuries, lost income, and reduced productivity. Governments pay less for police protection, judicial and legal proceedings, and compensation programs—costs that range in the hundreds of billions of dollars. Crime reduction also avoids the pain, suffering, and loss of quality of life that crime victims experience, the cost of which cannot be measured in dollars.

"D'Amico Perfect Choice to Straighten out Mess at State Parole Board," Arthur Z. Kamin, Asbury Park Press, July 9, 2003

In 2002, the New Jersey State Parole Board came under public scrutiny because it approved the early release of reputed mobster Angelo Prisco. Prosecutors had indicted Prisco for racketeering in 1994, and he went to state prison in 1998 on a 12-year sentence after pleading guilty to agreeing to pay a mob associate for torching a bar. The parole board denied him twice. He then hired a top Democratic law firm, one of whose partners allegedly contacted Governor James McGreevey's office. This time he secured parole. Federal and state investigations of this incident did not result in any indictments.

In the summer of 2002, however, the Chair of the Parole Board, Dr. Mario Paparozzi, abruptly resigned and moved to North Carolina, and William McCargo assumed the position of acting board chair. McCargo was under investigation for violation of conflict-of-interest rules and the hiring of a son-in-law and nephew for Parole Board jobs without the requisite qualifications. The newspapers labeled this situation "Parolegate.", an echo of "Watergate" the name given to a series of political scandals that occurred during the administration of US President Richard Nixon Kathy Ellis, Governor McGreevey's communications chief and the wife of my friend Ken Pringle, an attorney and mayor of Belmar, called me to ask if I would be interested in becoming the Chair. I was not looking for another job, but the situation presented an interesting challenge, so I agreed to think it over. After meeting with Parole Board Executive Director Michael Dowling and members of the Governor's administration to learn about the issues, I agreed to take the position. When announcing my appointment, Governor McGreevey said, "The Honorable John D'Amico has over 30 years of legal, public service and judicial experience to make him an effective chairperson.... I am confident that his judgments will prove to be fair, sound, and wise when determining an individual's eligibility for parole."

Reforming Parole

My first task was to work with the fourteen members of the Parole Board to define the mission and vision of the agency. The Board adopted a mission statement committing the agency "to promoting public safety and to fostering rehabilitation of offenders by implementing policies that result in effective parole case management." The Board also agreed that its "vision" should be "to improve the safety of the public and the quality of life in New Jersey." It would do this "by administering an innovative parole system that addresses the needs of the community, victims, and offenders through a responsible decision-making process that provides every available opportunity for successful offender reintegration."

There had to be an audit of the agency to uncover problems and set the stage for reforms. I asked Executive Director Dowling, Deputy Director Edward Bray, and Vice Chair Paul Contillo to conduct a comprehensive review of the Parole Board's policies and procedures. The Parole Board had been a dumping ground for favored political allies of former governors. Appointees to the Parole Board included former State Senators, three county party chairpersons, and former law enforcement officers. Many of them opposed parole reforms. Also appointed to the Board were two ministers who I had to restrain from self-dealing. One was steering parolees to a treatment center run by a relative regardless of their need for the services it provided. The other advocated a scheme under which inmates would be required to use the meager funds in their accounts to purchase credit cards from his company. Most troubling of all was a pending New Jersey State Commission of Investigation review of a board member's improper parole of two inmates as a favor for friends. He retired after I confronted him with the findings of the Commission. A hurricane destroyed his new Florida home the day after he acquired title to the property.

Because of the audit, I demoted three unqualified hearing officers who lacked the required college degree. One of them had been a former Jiffy Lube technician. I let five other hearing officers stay in their jobs provided that they earned their degrees within a certain time limit. News of these actions generated the editorial comment "way to go, Judge." [44]

Fortunately, I was able to convince a majority of Parole Board members to adopt many reforms and innovative programs. To restore public confidence, I had to ensure that parole decisions were based on facts and not influenced by external factors. I therefore required board members, hearing officers, and employees to reject requests for special treatment of parole eligible inmates. They had to inform the Executive Director or Deputy Director about any inquiries or recommendations regarding a parole case from outsiders like attorneys, legislators, or relatives. A Republican State Senator called me shortly after I implemented the procedure and requested the parole of one of his constituents. I declined and reported this inquiry to the Executive Director or Deputy Director. The senator was not pleased.

At my request, the Legislature gave civil service status to hearing officers. This protection freed them to make their parole recommendations impartially without outside pressure or undue influence and without fear of losing their jobs. The hearing officers reciprocated by working extra hours to clear a 6,000-case backlog of parole hearings that had accumulated under a prior chair.

We updated the Parole Handbooks for Adult and Young Adult Inmates to reflect new laws, rules, and processes. The Juvenile Unit improved parole supervision by revising its information systems, manuals, forms, and case review mechanisms. The Division of Parole created specialized units to supervise adult parolees. These units focus on Gang Reduction, Sex-offender Management, Electronic Monitoring, and Community Programs. A new Fugitive Unit led by Mark Lucia arrested Angelo Prisco in Delaware for leaving New Jersey without permission from his parole officer. Prisco went back to prison for the rest of his term.

To address complaints of racial discrimination, I requested an investigation and audit by the NJ Department of Personnel's Division of Equal Employment and Affirmative Action. Based on its recommendations, I introduced new management and personnel procedures to align with state policies on discrimination, harassment, and hostile work environment.

Another dysfunctional parole function involved county inmates. Inmates serving sentences of less than 364 days in county jails were not getting timely hearings. Deputy Executive Director Edward Bray solved this problem by allowing county jail inmates to waive initial parole hearings and proceed directly to final hearings. This reform helped many more inmates benefit from supervision, guidance, and placement in substance abuse and re-entry programs. It also saved counties over $2 million per year.

Another concern was that Parole board members needed more information to make proper determinations. I discovered that the statutory mandate to establish a risk assessment process had not been implemented. I secured funding for a new tool to evaluate offenders called the Level of Service Inventory—Revised, or LSI-R. It looks at factors like criminal history, substance abuse, mental health, relationships, family situation, and finances. Many states and Canada use it to predict if an inmate will commit another crime after being released.

Meeting the Challenge of Prisoner Reentry

In 2002, the New Jersey Institute for Social Justice and the New Jersey Public Policy Research Institute convened a Reentry Roundtable. It included policy makers, researchers, community and faith-based organizations, service providers and other key stakeholders. They gathered input, collected data, did research, analyzed policies, and reviewed the best learning available. In December 2003, the Roundtable released a report called "Coming Home For Good: Meeting the Challenge of Prisoner Reentry in New Jersey." Released five months after I became Chair, it painted a grim picture of prisoner re-entry in New Jersey:

> Almost all individuals incarcerated in the state of New Jersey — 95 to 97% — will eventually return home. They return, in large part, to poor and working-class urban New Jersey neighborhoods that are already under considerable social and economic strain. With disproportionately high rates of addiction, mental illness, and other serious health problems, as well as, on average, limited education, and work experience, returning prisoners must navigate a range of statutory and regulatory restrictions affecting their ability to get and keep employment, find stable housing, stay healthy and reintegrate into their families and communities. At present, most receive little to no preparation for the transition or for community living, and little to no support or assistance after they have been released. Following a growing trend over the past ten years, one third of those released last year had no parole supervision.[45]

The evidence gathered by the Roundtable showed that in the face of these challenges, most former prisoners would fail. In New Jersey, 60% of released inmates were rearrested within three years, with half of those arrests occurring within six months. Forty percent of all admissions to state prison were people who had failed on parole. NJ families, communities, and taxpayers were paying for the financial and social problems caused by the failure of prisoner reentry. We could not ensure public safety without addressing what was happening to parolees after release. They needed more help to overcome barriers they faced to become law-abiding and productive citizens.

I therefore proposed, and the Parole Board adopted, two major reforms of supervision procedures. The first reform sought to reduce the number of parolees returned to jail because of "technical" parole violations. Too many parole revocations were based on missing a meeting with a parole officer, violating a curfew, or failing a drug or alcohol test. The Parole Board adopted a new parole revocation procedure. Its guiding principle is that the response to a violation of a condition of parole should be proportional to the risk the parolee poses to the community. A parole officer must balance the severity of the violation alongside the potential for positive long-term outcomes. Parole officers should reschedule appointments if parolees cannot make them due to work conflicts, rather than sending them to jail. Instead of going back to prison, a parolee with a substance abuse relapse should get counseling and rehab at a halfway house or day reporting program.

The second major reform I presented was the Evidence-Based Supervision program. At the beginning of my leadership, I visited all the district parole offices seeking input about the parole supervision process. The most frequent complaint was that there was too much time devoted to paperwork and reports and not enough to help parolees succeed. So, I hired Dr. Faye Taxman to educate our district office supervisors about effective parole supervision procedures used in other states. Next, I formed a team of district supervisors and a representative from the parole officer's union to create a new supervision template.

The working group developed and proposed an Evidence-Based Supervision program. It uses the LSI-R risk assessment tool to guide prisoner reentry planning. Each parolee signs a case plan agreement outlining specific short-term and long-term goals broken down into manageable tasks such as securing housing, education, health care, and employment. Parole officers help in these efforts and use targeted sanctions and rewards to encourage progress toward the case plan goals. Compliant parolees receive less intensive supervision. Parole officers closely monitor parolees who are not making progress and send them to specialized residential and non-residential Parole Board Community Programs. These programs provide transitional rehabilitative programs that address substance abuse, mental illness, and/or job skills and readiness. Only persistent failures will cause the parolee's arrest and return to incarceration for violation of parole.

The unions representing the rank-and-file parole officers, the FOP, and the PBA, reacted negatively to these new procedures and sent letters to the Governor expressing a lack of confidence in my administration. Conservative "law and order" members of the Parole Board were also against them. Fortunately, I mustered just enough votes to secure approval by the Parole Board. Contrary to the predictions of their opponents, the two reforms had a positive impact. In 2005, The Philadelphia Inquirer reported that bucking a national trend, the state prison population in New Jersey had shrunk fourteen percent after reaching an all-time high of 31,000 in 1999. Among the reasons cited for the drop was the increase in the number of inmates paroled and the reduction of the number of parole violators sent back to prison from 5,400 to 2,900.

In addition to the reforms, I followed the advice of Kevin McHugh, the passionate and innovative former Director of Community Programs, and expanded the Parole Board's array of residential and day reporting programs. Thousands of parolees receive assistance with substance abuse, education, job readiness, and mental health through this program as a condition of parole at release or as an alternative to parole revocation and re-incarceration. These programs are essential components of an effective parole regime for three reasons. They work for most of the participants, cost less than incarceration, and represent the right thing to do to promote successful re-entry into society.

CRIMINAL JUSTICE COUNTDOWN

Although these reforms and the expanded community programs produced satisfactory results, I sensed that more needed to be done to increase successful offender re-entry. I therefore studied the issues related to recidivism and attended many conferences on the subject. I summed up what I learned in a compendium that I called the "Criminal Justice Count Down: 5-4-3-2-1":

Five

Criminal justice experts have identified five known predictors of offender recidivism: antisocial values, antisocial peers, poor self-control, family dysfunction, and past criminality. The absence of morals or values results in the inability of offenders to conform to the laws governing society and accepted notions of right and wrong.[46]

Four

Many studies identify four plagues of the criminal justice system: substance abuse, physical and mental illness, lack of education, and sexual predation.

Eighty percent of released inmates have a substance abuse problem. More than half of state prisoners report they were using drugs or alcohol when they committed the offense that led to their incarceration. One in five state prisoners say they committed their most recent crime to get money for drugs. The strategy of using prison as the primary solution for drug offenses has failed because the demand for drugs continues and new dealers take over. When drug treatment works, there are fewer customers. Treatment programs aimed at consumption reduction are much cheaper than prison. They reduce the likelihood of drug use and associated criminal behavior, and they increase employment. [47] The US Department of Health and Human Services, Centers for Disease Control estimates that every $1 invested in treatment reduces the costs of drug-related crime, criminal justice costs, and theft by $4 to $7. The total savings, with the addition of health care savings, can exceed costs by a ratio of twelve to one. [48]

Sadly, just one-fifth of former prisoners reintegrate into society through these programs. Nationwide, 15.6 percent of people aged twelve or older (or 43.7 million people) needed substance use treatment in 2021, but only 4.1 million people received any treatment. [49] Three in ten people under community supervision have substance use disorders, four times the rate of substance use disorders in the general population. Over two-thirds of probationers and parolees with substance use disorders report needing treatment, but not receiving it, and only one-third of people on community supervision with opioid use disorder receive medication-assisted treatment (MAT), the "gold standard[1]" of care. Program capacity needs to be expanded throughout the

---

1. https://pubmed.ncbi.nlm.nih.gov/25747920/

United States to serve people on parole and probation suffering from illicit drug or alcohol use disorders.[50]

One third of state prisoners have a learning or speech disability, hearing, or vision problem, or a mental or physical condition. About fifty percent of state prisoners suffer from at least one chronic condition, such as asthma, diabetes, or hypertension. Ten to seventeen percent have at least one communicable disease or condition, such as HIV, AIDS, tuberculosis, syphilis, chlamydia, gonorrhea, Hepatitis-B, or Hepatitis-C.[51] Parolees with untreated chronic diseases place substantial burdens on the community health system, particularly in terms of costly acute care and hospitalization. They also pose a threat to the health of the residents of the communities to which they return. Effective health planning for the return of ex-offenders to the community, specifically connecting them with community services, increases their chance of continuing to receive medical care. The Parole Board partnered with the US Department of Health and NJ Department of Health to help parolees access Federally Qualified Health Centers. The Parole Board, the NJ Department of Corrections, and US Social Security Administration agreed to speed up Medicaid applications for eligible NJ parolees. Much more needs to be done throughout the nation, however, to connect parolees with health coverage and care providers.

One in five people under community supervision has a mental health disorder, twice the rate of the general population. In New Jersey and other states, there is little or no sustained treatment for ex-offenders with mental health issues. The criminal justice system must manage their erratic behavior by default. As a result, mentally ill offenders move from hospitals to prisons and then to the streets, equipped with a limited supply of drugs They receive little or no care or guidance. Mentally ill parolees, particularly those with severe illness or co-occurring disorders (mental illness plus addiction to alcohol or drugs) have difficulty coping with the most basic reentry activities like finding housing and employment. As a result, they often commit new "crimes." Homeless people with mental disorders account for a significant percentage of arrested and incarcerated persons, and they often serve longer terms in prison than mentally healthy inmates with similar offenses.

We must identify mentally ill people in the criminal justice system and provide them with targeted services for self-determination and dignity after release. [52] The Parole Board developed a program to do so called the Program for Returning Offenders with Mental Illness Safely and Effectively (PROMISE). Operated by Volunteers of America Delaware Valley (VOADV) under the dedicated leadership of its Executive Director Dan Lombardo, it is located at Hope Hall in Camden, New Jersey. Parolees get a complete re-entry package from PROMISE, including psychiatric evaluation, individual and group mental health treatment, and medication monitoring. Treatment modalities include cognitive-behavioral intervention, motivational enhancement, relapse prevention therapy, and trauma-informed care. For residents capable of working, a job readiness program includes interview skills training and resumé help. PROMISE enrolls qualified individuals in the Supplemental Security Income program for people with disabilities. The program provides them with transitional housing until they can move into permanent supportive housing, where they hold their own leases and receive ongoing aftercare case management services. [53] In 2016, ex-offenders taking part in VOADV's programs had only a 19 percent re-incarceration rate three years post-release. [54] There should be more programs based on the PROMISE model in New Jersey and throughout the country.

The average level of education of prison inmates is sixth grade or lower. This is an unfortunate statistic because many inmates who have made bad life choices are highly intelligent. Lack of education and work skills are major impediments to meaningful employment and successful re-entry. We need to do a better job of encouraging parolees to pursue education in reading, writing, and math. Toward that end, the Parole Board encourages parolees to get GEDs. Vocational skills training programs are also extremely important. It is important to expand programs that match the changing needs of the workplace, like training in auto mechanics and culinary arts.

Sex offenders on parole pose exceedingly difficult supervisory problems. They are subject to restrictions regarding where they can live and with whom they can associate. The Parole Board's Sex-Offender Management Unit uses GPS electronic monitoring and polygraph (lie detector) testing to prevent parolees from violating their conditions of parole.

Three

The successful reintegration of parolees into society depends on society meeting three primary needs, namely jobs, housing, and transportation.

Research from both academics and practitioners suggests that the chief factor influencing the reduction of recidivism is an individual's ability to gain quality employment. Jobs prevent recidivism the same way hard time does. Every hour spent working is an hour a parolee does not have free to commit new crimes. Employed ex-prisoners support their families, contribute to their communities, provide for their own needs, and reclaim a sense of self-worth. Unfortunately, many parolees are unprepared for the competitive labor market upon release. They confront many barriers to employment, such as low education levels, stigma, statutory bars to certain occupations, and lost time from the labor force. Job applicants with a criminal record are less likely to be hired. The demand for parolees in blue-collar and manufacturing jobs has decreased. Parolees are not allowed to work in sectors like childcare, eldercare, customer service, and the service industry due to state laws and regulations.

Employers have strong incentives to hire parolees, such as federal bonding, tax breaks, and parole supervision protections. Also needed, however, is a concerted effort to educate, train, and help parolees to overcome the stigma of convict status so that they can secure and maintain living-wage jobs. The Parole Board and the NJ Department of Labor (DOL) created a simplified, automatic referral system by which each District Parole Office can connect parolees with the DOL One-Stop Career Center system. Parolees referred to One-Stop centers receive job readiness assessments, detailed remediation plans to help them become job ready, and job placement help. The Parole Board, NJ Department of Corrections, and US Social Security Administration agreed to speed up application processing for Supplemental Security Income and Food Stamps for parolees who cannot work. Other states should consider similar actions.

Housing is a key ingredient in successful reintegration. Successful reintegration depends on parolees having a safe place to live, especially during the critical first few months following release when returning prisoners fall back into old habits. Without stable housing, parolees struggle to meet basic needs, increasing their risk of relapse and reoffending. When I became Chair, thirteen hundred ex-prisoners per year were being released as "placement cases," meaning they had no place to live. Returning prisoners rarely have the financial resources or personal references necessary to compete for and secure housing in the private housing market. In most communities, a full-time minimum wage job does not cover the fair market rent for a two-bedroom apartment. In addition, landlords typically ask applicants to list employment and housing references and to disclose financial and criminal history information, which puts ex-offenders at a disadvantage.

For some parolees, returning to the homes of their families is not an option. Felony drug offenders are now ineligible for funding and housing due to welfare reform and public housing regulations. Moreover, federal housing policies can lead to the eviction of an entire household due to the criminal actions of a family member or guest. The Parole Board provides limited financial aid and temporary housing for parolees. Parolees need more help finding permanent housing and completing housing applications. They also need connections to community support systems that offer diverse services to assist with reentry.

One of the most troublesome problems parolees face is the restoration of driving privileges. Frequently, they lack the money with which to pay accumulated fines and surcharges. Parole Board representatives work in the prisons to help newly paroled inmates with discharge planning. One of their major tasks is to restore their driver's' licenses. Affordable access to public transportation is also critical.

Two

Both public and private sectors need to work together for successful prisoner re-entry. The Parole Board, representing the public sector, provides several residential and day reporting programs aimed at assisting offenders in the transition from prison to the street. The demand for these services exceeds program capacity, however. I therefore turned to the private sector for help by establishing a Community Partnership Unit at the Parole Board. I gave it the mandate to create new community-based partnerships with employers, labor unions, educational institutions, treatment and service providers, non-profit organizations, community groups, faith-based entities, foundations, individual volunteers, and mentors to promote successful prisoner re-entry.

One

There remained one fundamental problem in the criminal justice countdown. Twentieth-century entertainer Eddie Cantor articulated it: "When I see the *Ten Most Wanted Lists,* I always have this thought: If we had made them feel wanted earlier, they wouldn't be wanted now." When asked what the worst disease in the world was, Mother Teresa answered with one word: loneliness. When asked what we should do, she answered, "Let us touch... the poor, the lonely and the unwanted according to the graces we have received and let us not be ashamed or slow to do the humble work." Modern studies have examined loneliness and support this approach.[55]

Metamorphosis by Parole

The State Parole Board programs mentioned in the Criminal Justice Countdown are helpful, but they do not fully address the challenges of prisoner re-entry. To change the mindset and behavior of parolees, residential and day reporting programs in New Jersey and other states primarily use cognitive-behavioral therapy (CBT). CBT is a form of psychological treatment for a range of problems faced by parolees, including depression, anxiety disorders, substance abuse, marital discord, eating disorders, and severe mental illness. It is based on these core principles:

1. Psychological problems are based, in part, on faulty or unhelpful ways of thinking.

2. Psychological problems are based, in part, on learned patterns of unhelpful behavior.

3. People suffering from psychological problems can learn better ways to cope with them, relieving their symptoms and becoming more effective in their lives.

CBT focuses on what is going on in the person's current life, rather than what has led to his or her difficulties. The aim is to move forward in time to develop more effective ways of coping with problems through a change in thinking and behavioral patterns. Using role playing to prepare for potentially problematic interactions with others, as well as "homework" exercises, participants learn to face their fears instead of avoiding them. They learn to recognize thinking distortions that cause problems and how to reevaluate them based on reality. They improve their comprehension of other people's actions and intentions. They learn how to calm their minds, relax their bodies, and use problem-solving skills to cope with demanding situations. As a result, they develop a greater sense of confidence in their own abilities and become their own therapists. [56]

CBT has received national recognition as a "best practice" but has some limitations. Its effects are short term, and its narrow focus on providing quick diagnostics and treating symptoms is not a cure-all. Modern psychopharmacology (use of drugs to treat mental illness) can be helpful but requires a persistent adherence to prescription instructions. Some research questions the science behind selective serotonin reuptake inhibitors, a class of medications frequently prescribed to treat depression and anxiety. A new generation of social workers and psychologists is therefore resurrecting Freudian psychoanalysis and the talking cure. Critics have argued for years that psychoanalysis does not work, but data showing mixed evidence for the effectiveness of antidepressants undercut this argument. In addition, closer readings of Freud's writings are showing him to be more acceptable to feminists and the gay community. The major problem with psychoanalysis is that it is expensive and time consuming. [57]

Faith-Based Parole

I realized we needed a better remedy for the root causes of recidivism: behavioral dysfunction, antisocial values, poor self-control, lack of pro-social problem-solving skills, family dysfunction, the absence of morals or values, and the inability to conform to the laws governing society and accepted notions of right and wrong. Research is showing that delinquency, crime, and recidivism are inversely related to religious beliefs.[58] Faith-based programs can create the conditions for personal transformation and provide the inspiration necessary for successful re-entry. [59] I therefore concluded that for some parolees, a spiritual metamorphosis was required to defeat recidivism.

Saving former prisoners falls within the "mission field" of churches and faith-based organizations in the cities hardest hit by the cycle of imprisonment, release, and re-incarceration. I therefore reasoned that ministers, imams, priests, rabbis, and faith fellowship groups in these communities are uniquely qualified to help parolees replace antisocial values with pro-social values. Persons and communities of faith and compassion can counteract the negative and harmful influences of anti-social peers. They can also fill the emotional vacuum resulting from the absence of family support by treating parolees with respect, welcoming them into their families and communities, and helping them live lives of hope and purpose. They can teach ex-offenders to stop blaming someone or something else for their troubles and instead to accept, rather than deny, responsibility for their own actions. They can teach parolees they should not repeat past unacceptable behaviors. Their faith can convince parolees they are, spiritually speaking, new creations with new identities. As a result, they will find purpose and meaning in life and stay out of trouble.

Traditional public and nonprofit programs often cannot reach the most at-risk former prisoners in poor communities. The challenge was to encourage churches and faith-based institutions to provide necessary social, educational, and employment services. Fortunately, a famous Biblical passage opened the door: "Ask, and it will be given to you; seek, and you will find; knock and it will be opened to you." (Luke 11:10) Upon further inquiry I learned that many people of different faiths and their leaders were willing to help, but nobody had ever asked them. I therefore invited them, along with local law enforcement personnel, treatment providers, local officials, and interested citizens to Parole Board Community Partnership Conferences in or near New Jersey's major cities. There was no charge for food, drink, or participation. Co-sponsors, including schools, churches, and businesses, covered the costs.

Maurice "Bud" Scully, my former ally during the "Armour affair" at the Monmouth County Board of Social Services (Chapter 5), did a wonderful job leading the conferences. They featured workshops addressing the plagues and problems affecting former prisoners and their needs. After the sessions, I asked the attendees to join task forces and work on specific solutions. I put someone in charge of each task force to keep them going, provide info and resources, and make local connections.

I challenged the religiously affiliated conference attendees to respond to a "Parole Board altar call" to help combat immorality in the criminal justice mission field by changing the hearts and minds of at-risk former prisoners. They responded by joining the task forces. Their involvement led to the creation of a Bible-based Christian ministry called "The Most Excellent Way" (TMEW) (www.tmewcf.org). This program is a religious alternative to twelve step recovery programs like Alcoholics Anonymous and Narcotics Anonymous. It helps people within the church minister to parolees struggling with addiction through weekly Fellowship/Support meetings. The goal is to show participants love, acceptance, and forgiveness from God the Father, through Jesus Christ, and from peers. Ministers, priests, church leaders, and congregants throughout the State of New Jersey have embraced TMEW. It has become a powerful tool to help participants overcome their addictions. I explain how TMEW's ministry can be a powerful ally in the war on drugs in Chapter 8.

A major reason for the success of the New Jersey Parole Board's faith-based outreach has been the ability of the faith community to couple spiritual outreach and therapy with specific responses to the needs of ex-prisoners. Churches, charitable organizations such as the Salvation Army and Catholic Charities, community colleges, universities, municipal governments, and many individual volunteers have "answered prayers" by helping former prisoners. That help has taken the form of grants and loans for rental security deposits; temporary housing in unused church facilities and the homes of church members; job readiness training and referrals; transportation using church vehicles; restoration of drivers' licenses through donations to pay motor vehicle fines and insurance surcharges; donations of used vehicles; gifts of clothing, food, and furnishings; free haircuts and beauty treatments; and free medical and dental care.

These faith-based community outreach programs have worked wonders by garnering in-kind services, financial help, and donations for parolees worth millions of dollars—all at no cost to the taxpayers. While these benefits represented a tiny fraction of the state's corrections budget, they reflected a substantial involvement by the communities to which former prisoners return to help them overcome the challenges of re-entry. Unfortunately, the COVID-19 pandemic curtailed these programs. New Jersey and other states should not relinquish the benefits of community involvement.

While the community partnership conferences were taking place, the NJ Deputy Attorney General assigned to the Parole Board met with me. She pointed out that the Parole Board was a secular public agency, and she complained about the religious content of my speeches and presentations. She specifically took issue with my use of quotations from the Bible. I responded that the Parole Board was not promoting, encouraging, favoring, or proselytizing for any organization, religion, sect, or other faith-based belief system. Parole officers may not require former prisoners to take part in faith-based programs and initiatives, all such participation being voluntary. I thanked her for her advice and promised that I would change my speeches as soon as I received an injunction from a state or federal court. No injunction was forthcoming. Instead, Rev. Reginald T. Jackson, executive director of the Black Ministers Council of New Jersey said that the faith community had a "tremendous" responsibility to keep former prisoners "from turning around and going right back to prison." He added that government should not be shy about asking religious organizations to help getting prisoners ready for release because "there are some things we can do better than government can."[60]

At the end of my term as Chair of the Parole Board in 2007, I left the agency with policies and procedures in place that would bring good news in the years that followed. A major issue is unresolved, however. One third of inmates released from state prisons annually "max out" without parole supervision.

These inmates either opt to serve their complete sentence to avoid parole supervision or are denied parole because of their misconduct in prison. We should not release these prisoners without supervision or transitional support.

Thousands of max outs leave prison in New Jersey and in other states after extended periods of incarceration burdened by serious criminal records, substance abuse addictions, chronic physical and/or mental health problems, limited education, poor job skills, and little or no family support. They go back to cities like Newark and Camden in large numbers, causing more crime, public health risks, and homelessness. Most of them get no help with the arduous task of successful reentry into society. They have no case plans, goals, manageable tasks, and they are not subject to rules, curfews, or random drug testing. They are ineligible to take part in the Parole Board's residential and day-reporting Community Programs and receive no reentry services. [61]

A 2007 Parole Board study showed that prisoners who completed their sentence were more likely to be re-convicted and re-incarcerated than parolees. In 2013, the Pew Charitable Trusts studied New Jersey data and came to the same conclusion—namely, that even when controlling for risk factors such as an offender's prior record that reliably predict recidivism, parolees have better public safety outcomes than inmates who serve their full sentences. The data from offenders released in 2008 revealed that parolees had better public safety outcomes than max outs. Fewer of them were arrested, reconvicted, or returned to prison for a new crime within three years of release. Unfortunately, between fiscal years 2017 and 2020 two-member Parole Board panels paroled only an average of 48% of the inmates appearing at their hearings. [62] These denials were based on subjective gut instincts and fear of chastisement if an inmate they paroled were to commit a new crime. Board members focused on discrepancies between the criminal offenses charged in indictments and the crimes to which inmates had pleaded guilty by agreement between prosecutors and defense attorneys. They would make favorable parole decisions only if the inmates "didn't scare" them. I argued they should instead base their decisions on objective factors such as behavior in prison, psychological evaluations, and risk and needs assessment information.

New Jersey took a major step forward along these lines in 2021 by adopting the "Earn Your Way Out" Act. Originally sponsored by former State Senator Raymond Lesniak, the law[2] requires the state Department of Corrections to develop reentry plans for inmates to ease their transition out of prison. Upon entering the prison system, hearing officers prepare plans for the inmates that serve as a road map for participation in counseling, education, and other programs to help improve their lives once they leave. Inmates who have not committed violent crimes or sex offenses and have a clean disciplinary record for two years prior to their parole eligibility date are paroled administratively if they have completed required rehabilitation programs. Inmates are also eligible for administrative parole if they are unable to participate in these programs due to circumstances beyond their control, like program capacity or exclusionary policies. [63] This reform will cause the release of many more inmates on parole. Paroling authorities in other states should consider it. New Jersey and other states also need to expand and improve in-prison rehab programs for better results in reducing recidivism.

New Jersey has failed, however, to adhere to another reform needed to realize the full benefits of supervised prisoner re-entry. During my testimony at the Assembly Regulatory Oversight Committee in January 2006, I suggested incorporating parole supervision into every state prison sentence, as advised by experts, and supported by studies. Sponsored by Congresswoman Bonnie Watson Coleman when she was in the State Assembly, New Jersey enacted such an early release law in 2011. It required the release of all eligible state inmates to parole supervision at least six months before the expiration of their sentences. Governor Chris Christie repealed the law less than a year later due to two former prisoners committing murders after early release. The DOC did not place them in a halfway house, nor did they come under parole supervision because DOC neglected to release them directly to parole officers. Had that been done, the murders might not have happened.

Pew Charitable Trust studies in New Jersey and other states show that if the early release law had remained in place since 2011, fewer crimes would have been committed. More former prisoners would also have gotten the help they

2. https://www.njleg.state.nj.us/2018/Bills/PL19/364_.HTM

need. Daryl's case illustrates the point. Sentenced for murder as a young adult, he called state prison home for 30 years. Like over half of prisoners in New Jersey, he served his entire sentence and left prison without any post-release help. Had Daryl been paroled, the Parole Board could have sent him to a residential community program. That program would have helped him find employment and housing. Absent referral to a halfway house, his parole officer could have helped him find transitional housing. Instead, Daryl returned to a neighborhood he no longer recognized. His only possessions were his birth certificate and social security card. He had left the structure of a prison environment that told him what to wear, when and what to eat, and when and where to sleep. Now he was roaming the streets of a city where he knew no one and had no resources. Reluctant to go to a shelter, he slept in doorways and at the bus station during snowstorms. During a Code Blue blizzard emergency, the police took him, along with all other unsheltered homeless persons, to a shelter. It was there, at last, that Daryl was finally referred to a reentry program where he got the help he needed. Max outs less fortunate than Daryl often resort to desperate measures, including crime, to survive.

Besides reducing crime, paroling all inmates before expiration of their sentences can save enormous amounts of money. For example, in New Jersey, if the 2017 cohort of 6,000 annual max-outs had been paroled six months early, the New Jersey DOC would have saved $22,075 per inmate net after the cost of parole, and the total annual savings in the DOC budget after the first phase in year would have approximated $132 million. Placing all inmates on parole at release could generate huge savings in other states as well. [64]

While Chair, I was fortunate to hire my good friend Robert Kantor as a hearing officer. We nicknamed him "Saint Robert" for his ability to solve tough cases involving treatment and placement of parolees. My successors wisely assigned Robert to the Community Programs Unit, where he supervised the continuation of the regional task forces that arose from the Community Partnership Conferences. Robert produced the idea to use libraries throughout the state to provide reentry resources and support for parolees returning to their local communities upon completion of their prison terms. Under this program, called "Fresh Start," social workers conduct individualized assessments of parolees and provide referrals to employment opportunities, library resources, and online occupational skills training.

In 2014, former Governor James McGreevey started the New Jersey Reentry Corporation. NJRC works with the Parole Board to give participants personalized assessments and treatment plans that cover important needs like housing, medical care, and health insurance. NJRC welcomes both parolees and max-outs and has achieved remarkable results with its focus on job training, employment counseling, and employment placement. [65] A program worth emulating nationwide!

After I retired from the Parole Board in 2007, the National Institute of Corrections, US Department of Justice, invited me to join a group of parole authorities and corrections practitioners to create a monograph. Its goal was to help parole authorities make "evidence-based" release decisions and fashion effective supervisory policies and procedures. Practices are "evidence-based" if supported by research supporting desired outcomes and measurable results. Our report recommended as best practices the use of risk and needs assessments such as the LSI-R, motivational interviewing techniques, and targeted interventions—all of which had been embraced by the NJ Parole Board. The report also cited research showing that supervision and treatment services focused on lower-risk offenders produce little net positive effect on recidivism rates. To enhance public safety, it urged paroling authorities to target resources to higher-risk offenders. [66] The New Jersey Parole Board has incorporated these principles in its decision making and supervision operations. Other states should do so as well. They should also consider adding faith-based parole programs, like those in New Jersey, as a voluntary option for parole supervision.

Ministers, priests, imams, and members of the faith-based community are continuing to work for the salvation of formerly incarcerated sinners. Their hard work and that of the dedicated employees of the Parole Board and the citizens who collaborated with it in their communities during and after my tenure as Parole Board chair have produced miraculous results. A 2018 study by the National Reentry Resource Center and the Council of State Governments

Justice Center found that New Jersey's recidivism rate fell from 60 percent in 2001 to 37 percent by 2007 and to 29.8 percent in 2013. It attributed these gains to changes in the state parole system and increases in the state's offerings of residential and community-based programs for parolees to help them stay on track and transition back successfully to life outside prison. Also cited were programs fostering general rehabilitation, treating substance abuse, and managing mental illness. [67]

This success proves that for persons convicted of crimes, properly and effectively administered parole can bring about the metamorphosis described by the Apostle Paul in Ephesians 4:22-24: "that you put off, concerning your former conduct, the old man which grows corrupt according to the deceitful lusts, and be renewed in the spirit of your mind, and that you put on the new man which was created according to God, in true righteousness and holiness."

Chapter 8: Religion and the War on Drugs

No temptation has overtaken you except such as is common to man; but God is faithful, who will not allow you to be tempted beyond what you are able, but with the temptation will also make the way of escape, that you may be able to bear it.

—-1 Corinthians 10:13

Monmouth County's battle against substance abuse was a critical issue when I was a County Commissioner in the 1980's. The influx of "crack" cocaine into Monmouth County overwhelmed treatment programs, causing waiting lists for new patients. I proposed a four-point program:

1. Emergency funding for substance abuse agencies to beef up their education, public information, early intervention, and prevention programs.
2. Increased funding for a "Crack Kills" campaign with cooperation and coordination among the County Board of Drug Abuse Services, Alcoholism Services Board, Mental Health Board, the prosecutor's office, superintendents of schools, and other agencies—the first such effort in the state.
3. Additional comprehensive substance abuse education and prevention programs.
4. Increased funding for outpatient and inpatient treatment services, including development of acute care beds and expansion of residential care facilities.

Charles Brown, director of Monmouth County's Drug Abuse Services, warned that the fight against drug use would require substantial dollars, saying, "we can either pay now, or pay later." This maxim continues to ring true today.

Over time, the crack cocaine epidemic abated, but a new plague has taken its place. The National Institute on Drug Abuse reports that over 106,000 died in 2021 from overdoses of illicit drugs and prescription opioids. The number of overdose deaths involving synthetic opioids, specifically fentanyl, rose to 70,601 that year. Overdose deaths from stimulants like cocaine and methamphetamine rose to 32,537 in 2021. [68]

For every drug overdose that results in death, there are many more nonfatal overdoses, each one with its own emotional and economic toll. As I pointed out in the "Criminal Justice Countdown" in Chapter 7, pervasive substance abuse plagues the criminal justice system. It also burdens family courts. Drug and alcohol addiction causes child and spousal abuse, violent crime, rape, teen pregnancy, sexually transmitted diseases, family breakup, divorce, school dropout, debilitating accidents, and job loss.

The prescriptions for addressing this plague resemble those employed in the campaign against crack: expanded distribution and use of naloxone; overdose prevention education; expanded awareness about, access to, and availability of treatment for substance use disorders; and early intervention with individuals at highest risk of overdose. Early intervention and treatment for substance use disorders offer substantial benefits. Like other chronic diseases, we can manage addiction successfully by providing access to quality treatment. We can use early intervention tools in existing systems like primary care and hospitals to respond quickly to substance use disorders and help more people. The overarching goal of treatment should be to help individuals achieve stable, long-term recovery and become productive members of society. In the process, we can eliminate the public health, public safety, and economic consequences associated with addiction. [69]

The demand for substance abuse treatment exceeds the capacity of non-profit and government-funded programs. For those who graduate from treatment programs, the rate of relapse is discouragingly high. Meanwhile, federal and state governments are spending millions of dollars on criminal justice measures such as drug interdiction, criminal prosecution, and incarceration that are widely regarded as a failure. [70]

Recognizing that addiction is a chronic disease, the New Jersey Department of Human Services has implemented a program called "Recovery Management Check-Up (RMC) Service" to deal with the problem of relapses. This federally funded program provides monthly check-ins for persons who have completed treatment. They can talk to treatment experts in person, by phone, through virtual meetings, text messaging, and online chats. Counselors assess clients using motivational interviewing techniques and a brief assessment tool to evaluate their progress, needs, and recovery status. They will connect clients with community resources like self-help meetings, food pantries, and sober houses. The staff will admit them to a residential treatment program if necessary. The goal of RMC is to enable those in recovery to remain in recovery. [71]

While serving as Chairperson of the New Jersey State Parole Board, I discovered and introduced a long-term intervention program that helped many parolees. I found a report from the National Center on Addiction and Substance Abuse at Columbia University stating that spirituality can play a powerful role in the prevention and treatment of substance abuse and in the maintenance of sobriety. It asserted that because religion gives meaning and purpose to life, religious people are less likely to abuse drugs and alcohol. Doctors and addiction experts suggest that prayer, meditation, and spiritual experiences satisfy mental and physical needs, promote a sense of belonging and purpose, and function as a protective factor in preventing and recovering from addiction. [72]

I therefore added the Most Excellent Way (TMEW) ministry as a voluntary religious option to Alcoholics Anonymous (AA) and Narcotics Anonymous (NA) programs for parolees suffering from substance abuse. TMEW provides group counseling on alternatives to chemical dependency with an emphasis on the redemptive power of faith. [73] It focuses on a process of permanent change of compulsive habits and self-centered behavior from the inside out—as a matter of the heart. It encourages self-examination, mental renewal, and spiritual transformation based on ten "Attitudes of Victorious Living":

1. Humility: I admit I am powerless over the effects of drugs and alcohol, and self-centered behavior — my life is unmanageable. Jesus said: "Blessed are the poor in spirit, for theirs is the kingdom of heaven." Matthew 5:3

2. Repentance: I believe Jesus Christ can and will create in me a new way of life. Jesus said: "Blessed are those who mourn, for they shall be comforted." Matthew 5:4

3. Submissiveness: I give my will and my life to Jesus Christ. Jesus said: "Blessed are the meek, for they shall inherit the earth." Matthew 5:5

4. Honesty: I honestly examine myself in the light of God's Word. Jesus said: "Blessed are those who hunger and thirst for righteousness, for they shall be filled." Matthew 5:6

5. Mercy: I humbly ask God's forgiveness for my sinful past. I am able to forgive those who have hurt me. Jesus said: "Blessed are the merciful, for they shall obtain mercy." Matthew 5:7

6. Obedience: I desire to live under the guidance of God's Holy Spirit, day by day. Jesus said: "Blessed are the pure in heart, for they shall see God." Matthew 5:8

7. Reconciliation: I ask forgiveness from God and those I have hurt or dealt with unfairly. Jesus said: "Blessed are the peacemakers, for they shall be called sons of God." Matthew 5:9

8. Faith: I trust in the power of Jesus Christ when I face hardship and trials. Jesus said: "Blessed are those who are persecuted for righteousness' sake, for theirs is the kingdom of heaven." Matthew 5:10

9. Perseverance: I stand firm in my faith that Jesus is in control of all things. Jesus said: "Blessed are you when they revile and persecute

you and say all kinds of evil against you falsely for My sake. Rejoice and be exceedingly glad, for great is your reward in heaven, for so they persecuted the prophets who were before you." Matthew 5:11-12

10. Loving Service: As a new creation in Christ, I share with others the Good News of a risen Savior who makes His people whole. Jesus said: "You are the salt of the earth; ... You are the light of the world ... Let your light so shine before men, that they may see your good works and glorify your Father in heaven." Matthew 5:13-16

The New Jersey State Parole Board's experience with TMEW was positive. Few parolees dropped out of the program, and the recidivism rate of successful completes was exceptionally low; therefore, the New Jersey courts gave TMEW the same official acceptance accorded to AA and NA. I attribute these remarkable results to an environment in which participants can freely express their faith and grow in fellowship with others through support groups. As the Re-Entry Policy Council has observed, "The example of others who have faced similar challenges and succeeded, the permission to talk about personal issues with and form attachments to a group of peers, a sense of religious faith, or other forms of inspiration can support an individual's mental resolve to complete a rigorous substance abuse treatment regimen, to get and maintain a job, or to manage family conflicts peacefully." [74]

A thorough study conducted in 2019 found that faith plays a significant role in preventing and recovering from substance abuse. Religious beliefs and practices, along with spiritual programs inspired by faith, can help address issues that medical interventions alone may not resolve. Congregations and faith-based institutions are good at mobilizing communities and responding quickly to crises. They are highly capable of facilitating group interactions that address past negative experiences, which can lead to mental illness and substance abuse. Congregational volunteer addiction recovery groups in the US save the economy $316.6 billion per year without using taxpayer money. The study found that religion and spirituality are powerful tools in substance abuse prevention and recovery. Faith plays a key role in treating the mind, body, and spirit. For these reasons, the decline in religious affiliation in the USA is a national health concern.[75]

MURDER, MEDIA, AND METAMORPHOSIS

Chapter 9: Preventing the Murder of Planet Earth

But now ask the beasts, and they will teach you; And the birds of the air, and they will tell you; Or speak to the earth, and it will teach you; And the fish of the sea will explain to you. Who among all these does not know that the hand of the Lord has done this, in whose hand is the life of every living thing, And the breath of all humankind?

—-Job 12:7-10

Humankind is committing a global murder/suicide. In 2023, a prestigious group of European scientists warned that six out of nine of the Earth's "planetary boundaries", or life support systems, have been so damaged that the planet is "well outside the safe operating space for humanity." By causing pollution and destroying the natural world, humans have broken the limits of key global systems needed to maintain a healthy planet. The systems beyond safe limits include carbon dioxide produced by global warming, the health of ecosystems, quantity and quality of freshwater, flow of nitrogen and phosphorus, loss of forests, and synthetic pollution from pesticides, plastics, and nuclear waste. Two planetary boundaries at risk of being breached are air pollution and ocean acidification. The only one out of danger is atmospheric ozone.[76] These are not irreversible tripping points, but they are red flags demanding action.

Despite my past connections to notorious murders in New Jersey, I never expected to play a role confronting the attempted murder of our planet decades later. In 2005, an FBI investigation called "Operation Bid Rig" led to charges against eleven former county and municipal officials. The United States Attorney for the District of New Jersey, Former New Jersey Governor Christopher Christie, said in a December 6, 2006, news release that "the corruption that has existed in Monmouth County is stunning and wide in scope." Harry Larrison, the longest serving Director of the Board of County

Commissioners, was the most prominent official charged. Christie accused him of accepting $8,500 from two developers for help in moving their projects forward. Larrison died a month before standing trial. Eight other defendants pled guilty to an assortment of bribery, money-laundering, and extortion charges. Two cases went to trial. The defendants were convicted, fined, and incarcerated.

The Republican Party controlled the Board of County Commissioners during the two decades following my departure in 1988. Because of "Operation Bid Rig," wasteful spending, and cronyism, it earned the nickname "Club Monmouth." This adverse publicity helped Barbara McMorrow, then a Democrat, win a seat on the Board of County Commissioners in 2006. I had the honor of swearing her in. Democratic Chair Vic Scudiery invited me to run for county commissioner in 2007. The Asbury Park Press endorsed me, stating that "voters sick of corruption, patronage politics, and wasteful spending should give Democrats the opportunity to do what the current board has refused to do—institute meaningful reform." Out of nine legislative and four county offices at stake, I was the only Democrat to win by the extremely close margin of 394 votes out of over 120,000 votes cast.

IN 2008, DEMOCRATIC County Commissioner Amy Mallett rode to victory on the Democratic wave created by the election of President Barack

Obama. As a result, in 2009, the Democratic party gained control of the Board for the first time since 1985. It lasted only one year.

During the year we were in charge, we enacted a code of ethics, adopted the state's first county strategic plan, started shared services with municipalities and school districts, expanded Economic and Workforce Development Department programs, targeted budget savings, and reformed bidding processes. We also created an in-house Law Department. Before losing control, the Republicans tried to transfer the Board's powers to their hand-picked County Administrator. We rolled back this illegal attempt to change the form of the Monmouth Couty government without voter approval.

Thinking Green

When I returned to the county government, my top priority was to reduce river pollution, protect open space, and help towns improve their parks. County Commissioner McMorrow and I started a lunchtime series to encourage discussions about the environment, share green ideas, and provide information on eco-friendly choices. In our first session, we presented ideas for improving the environmental friendliness, energy efficiency, and occupant health of both old and new buildings. We highlighted a building design certification program called Leadership in Energy and Environmental Design (LEED) that has become a national standard for developing sustainable green buildings. To earn LEED certification, a building project must use sustainable strategies in areas such as energy efficiency, water savings, building materials, indoor environment, location, and transportation. Levels of certification include silver, gold, and platinum. [77]

Another session featured helpful energy saving suggestions for homeowners and renters. Lighting accounts for around fifteen percent of an average home's electricity use. Households can save a lot of money by using LED lighting. LEDs use as much as 90% less energy and last up to twenty-five times longer than traditional incandescent bulbs. They are also more efficient than fluorescent light bulbs. We also urged homeowners and renters to fight "vampire loads" or "phantom power" to reduce energy use and lower electricity bills. Modern televisions, computers, phones, stereos, microwaves, and coffeemakers continue to draw electricity even when not in use if they remain plugged in. Plugging these appliances into power strips and switching them off when not in use can save energy and money. Smart power strips can detect when a device is in standby mode and will automatically cut power off to save energy.

Global Warming

The measures we advocated at the environmental luncheons were small but important. We need global efforts to save the Earth from the most polluting industries, like fossil fuels, agriculture, fashion, food retail, transport, and construction. To survive, we must decarbonize these industries. [78] When I began my third term as a County Commissioner in 2008, I was aware of an increasing "planetary emergency" because of the dangers of global warming highlighted by former Vice President Al Gore's 2006 movie, "An Inconvenient Truth." Winner of an Academy Award, the documentary showed how human interaction with the natural environment since the Industrial Revolution had caused carbon dioxide (CO_2) levels to increase and raise the planet's average temperature. This has resulted in melting glaciers, higher ocean temperatures, stronger storms, and the appearance of other threats to life as we know it. The film showed that human activity contributes to global warming. We can stop and reverse it by choosing green options like using less electricity, buying eco-friendly cars, and being mindful of our purchases.

In 2007, the Intergovernmental Panel on Climate Change (IPCC), established by the World Meteorological Organization and the United Nations Environment Program, issued its Fourth Assessment Report on Climate Change. It summarized six years of research by over 2,500 scientists from over 130 countries. It found that global warming was unequivocal. Energy supply, transport, industry, and land-use changes had contributed significantly to the increase in greenhouse gas emissions between 1970 and 2004. As a result, rising air and ocean temperatures were causing widespread melting of snow and ice, sea level rise, more frequent and intense floods, and longer lasting droughts. There was more coastal erosion. Plants and animal species were going extinct. Severe weather events were more frequent and intense, and millions of people were experiencing adverse health impacts because of climate change-related exposures.

The report stated that adaptation and mitigation would be necessary to address impacts resulting from the warming that had already occurred because of past emissions, and it predicted that greenhouse gas emissions would continue to grow over the next few decades unless there were changes in lifestyle and behavior patterns. Recommendations included using cars less, using technology to reduce CO2 emissions from buildings, adopting agricultural practices to increase soil carbon storage, reducing greenhouse gas emissions, stopping deforestation, and preserving natural habitats. The report recommended raising the price of carbon to encourage investments in low-greenhouse gas emission products, technologies, and processes. [79]

While the IPCC report had a worldwide focus, it was clear that state, county, and municipal governments had to play a part in addressing global warming. My experience on the Monmouth County Board of Commissioners showed me that counties can address greenhouse gas emissions by improving transportation, conserving energy, and water, and managing wastewater and solid waste disposal more efficiently. The economic arguments for implementing climate stabilization solutions were compelling, from near-term gains of energy efficiency and reduced electric bills to long-term climate protection initiatives. It all added up to reducing the impact of greenhouse gas emissions.

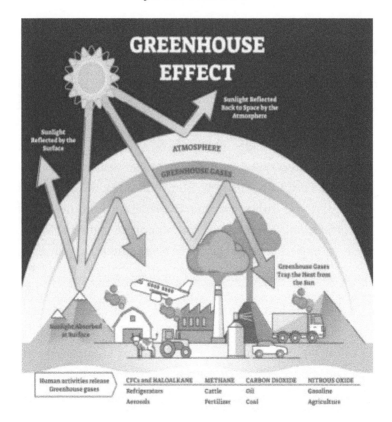

I THEREFORE SPONSORED a resolution creating a Greenhouse Gas (GHG) Reduction Advisory Committee tasked with developing a GHG Reduction Plan for Monmouth County. The aim of the program was to reduce energy costs and develop alternative sources of energy. Additional goals involved preserving open space and farmland, improving land-use policies, using LEED standards in new construction, and rehabilitating county buildings. The GHG Committee would strive to improve air quality, promote waste-to-energy programs, and expand public transportation. I hoped that this initiative would move Monmouth County toward energy independence, save taxpayer money, and enable the county to take advantage of state and federal incentives and grants. It would also burnish the county's reputation as a community of choice by improving its quality of life. The Board of Commissioners adopted the resolution unanimously.

The Board appointed government, business, and science professionals to the GHG Reduction Advisory Committee and gave them these tasks:

- Create an inventory of the county's operational greenhouse gas emissions.
- Develop policies, programs, and operations to achieve significant measurable and sustainable reduction of greenhouse gas emissions.
- Recommend steps to achieve New Jersey's climate stabilization goals by promoting energy efficiency in county facilities.
- Recommend steps for towns to take to reduce emissions and increase energy efficiency.
- Share ideas with local, state, and federal governments and other stakeholders about how to achieve New Jersey's climate stabilization goals.

Some fruits of these labors included a gas-to-energy program at the county's garbage dump, known as the Reclamation Center, which harnessed methane gas produced naturally by decomposing garbage and converted it into electricity. The county Department of Public Works switched to biodiesel fuel for its vehicle fleet. The Highway Department replaced rock salt treated with calcium with magnesium chloride, which is easier to apply and biodegradable. A roundtable energy forum sponsored by the Commissioners educated towns and residents about the sustainable and efficient renewable energy options available for private homes and public buildings.

I rejoined the North Jersey Transportation Planning Authority (NJTPA) as the Monmouth County Commissioner representative and secured its approval in 2009 for a first-of-a-kind study about steps the county could take to reduce its transportation-related carbon footprint. Managed by the Monmouth County Planning Board, it had these objectives:

- Evaluate how trends such as climate change, travel pattern changes, and rising energy and commuting costs would impact the way people travel in Monmouth County.
- Review the county government's transportation-related greenhouse

gas emissions and recommend short- and long-term strategies for reducing them.

- Develop strategies to reduce county employees' and residents' vehicle miles traveled (VMT) including support for bicycling, walking and transit facilities; and
- Develop "toolboxes" to help municipalities reduce their transportation related GHG emissions.

Inspired by the NJTPA study, I sponsored the state's first "Complete Streets" resolution to encourage people to move around Monmouth County without automobiles, which generate substantial greenhouse gas emissions. It requires all county-funded road, bridge, and building projects to include plans for sidewalks, bike lanes, safe crossings, and transit amenities wherever possible. It gives municipalities similar guidelines, recommending paved shoulders in new road construction and reconstruction projects. In cities and densely populated suburban towns, it recommends bus lanes, curb ramps, crosswalks, countdown pedestrian signals, curb extensions, pedestrian-scale lighting, and bike lanes. The Complete Streets program has made it easier for pedestrians and bicyclists to get to places of employment, educational institutions, retail establishments, transit centers, recreational facilities, and public offices. [80]

Because of my work on environmental initiatives, I was invited in 2008 to take part in a historic climate action meeting at the Pocantico Center at the Rockefeller estate near Tarrytown, New York. With support from the Rockefeller Brothers Fund, fifty mayors and county commissioners formed a coalition of local governments called "Climate Communities." Its aim was to develop a "Blueprint for Local Climate Action" to present to the incoming Obama Administration.

The Blueprint noted that local governments across the country are the first responders who must deal with the impacts of climate change, including drought, water shortages, wildfires, flooding, rising sea levels, and economic shifts and impacts. It stated that local governments could promote green infrastructure that reduces carbon emissions by preserving open space, implementing waste-to-energy programs, and incorporating LEED certification in construction. It added that local governments should implement economic development strategies to create green businesses and green jobs. Toward those ends, the Blueprint requested funding from the Small Business Administration, Department of Housing and Urban Development, and other agencies for local green business development.

The Blueprint also advocated a national market-based cap-and-trade policy that would set limits on greenhouse gas emissions. The government would set a cap on carbon dioxide and related global warming emissions across an industry, or ideally, the entire economy. There would be penalties for violations of the cap, which would gradually get stricter. A trade market would allow companies to buy and sell allowances, allowing them to emit only a certain amount of greenhouse gases, with supply and demand setting the price. Trading would give companies a powerful incentive to save money by cutting emissions in the most cost-effective ways. The Blueprint estimated that the carbon market would generate $150 billion in new revenue per year. It proposed using this money to help local governments reduce greenhouse gas emissions by funding conservation, transportation improvements, green technologies, and clean energy projects.

For the second time in my career, I went to Washington, DC, to lobby for federal legislation. I joined six dozen mayors, county officials and other members of Climate Communities for meetings with senators, congresspeople, and representatives of the Obama Administration to promote the Blueprint for Local Climate Action. We achieved one major success and suffered one major failure. The success was the inclusion of $90 billion for counties and cities to use on ready to go clean energy capital projects in the economic stimulus bill signed by President Obama in 2009. Monmouth County received over $18 million in federal grants from this program which it used to install energy efficient boilers and chillers in county buildings, repair a dam and two bridges, resurface forty miles of roadway, and install new LED technology in forty traffic signals. County Commissioner Amy Mallet oversaw a 1.4-megawatt solar energy project that placed solar panels on the roofs of five county buildings and over a large parking lot, reducing the county's electricity bill by over $3 million per year. Other New Jersey counties also received "green" funding.

The failure was the demise of the comprehensive Waxman-Markey climate bill, which would have established a national cap-and-trade system for limiting emissions. The bill passed the House in June 2009 but died in the Senate. Notwithstanding this defeat, the Obama Administration implemented several important energy conservation measures. It agreed with auto companies on improved fuel economy standards, a step the industry had resisted for 25 years. The Environmental Protection Administration tackled truck emissions and reined in methane leaks from the oil and gas industry. The Department of Energy updated energy efficiency standards for home appliances like fridges, washers, dryers, and freezers. President Joe Biden's administration continued to strengthen these programs.

New Jersey, Connecticut, Delaware, Maine, Maryland, Massachusetts, New Hampshire, New York, Rhode Island, and Vermont formed a Regional Greenhouse Gas Initiative (RGGI) in 2005. This consortium of states put regional limits on carbon dioxide emissions from power plants and created a cap-and-trade market allowing utility companies to buy and sell permits to pollute. Over six years, the program had reduced average utility bills by 3.4 percent across the Northeast[1], driven the reinvestment of $2.7 billion[2] in revenues into public projects, and created at least 30,200 new jobs[3]. Unfortunately, former Governor Chris Christie withdrew New Jersey from the compact in 2011.

Fortunately, Christie's successor, Governor Phil Murphy, resurrected New Jersey's response to global warming and climate change with a series of measures worthy of emulation in other states. In 2018, he renewed New Jersey's membership in the RGGI compact, arguing that Governor Christie's withdrawal from it "lacked any common sense," left money on the table, and "robbed" New Jersey of the opportunity to invest in clean energy options. The proceeds from New Jersey's renewed participation in the RGGI are being

---

1. http://acadiacenter.org/wp-content/uploads/2016/07/
   Acadia_Center_2016_RGGI_Report-Measuring_Success_FINAL_08092016.pdf

2. http://www.rggi.org/docs/Auctions/36/PR060917_Auction36.pdf

3. http://www.analysisgroup.com/uploadedfiles/content/insights/publishing/
   analysis_group_rggi_report_july_2015.pdf

invested in electric buses, trucks, passenger vehicles, and charging station installations.

In 2012, California established a cap-and-trade program setting a limit on climate pollution, covering 80% of the state's emissions. The limit declines every year and regulated businesses—large electric power plants, industrial factories, and fuel distributors—must either reduce their pollution or pay for so-called emissions allowances. California and Quebec link their markets, enabling them to combine their supply of allowances and conduct joint auctions.[81] California is also considering a link with Washington State. Over ten years, California dramatically reduced its emissions, grew its economy, raised $23 billion for environment and public health programs, and serves as a model for other states looking to combat climate change by charging polluters.[82]

In 2021, New Jersey Governor Phil Murphy signed an executive order establishing an interim greenhouse gas reduction target of 50 percent below 2006 levels by 2030 and a 100 percent reduction in greenhouse gas emissions by 2050. He signed additional executive orders in 2023, putting in place zero-emission heating and cooling systems in a half-million homes and businesses by 2030 and banning the sale of gasoline-fueled vehicles by 2035. California, New York, Oregon, Vermont, and Massachusetts have also passed rules banning the sale of new gas-powered cars by 2035. If you share my concern about the dangers of global warming, urge your state and local governments to adopt similar programs.

Hurricanes and Floods

I had witnessed beach erosion at the Jersey Shore since I was a child. Houses and roads washed into the ocean in hurricanes and strong coastal storms called "nor'easters." Over four decades, legislators, regulators, planners, and environmentalists tried to limit development in vulnerable coastal areas. The powerful developer's lobby effectively blocked these efforts. When I was in the Senate in 1989, I sponsored a Natural Resources Protection Trust fund bill that would raise about $35 million a year for shore protection, park restoration, open space acquisition, and flood control. Although the bill establishing the trust fund passed the Senate, the second bill to provide the money by small increases in the realty transfer tax and a two percent tax increase on hotel and motel rooms failed in the face of unanimous Republican opposition. Ill-advised development continued with little effort to bolster shore protection, with disastrous consequences.

Notwithstanding the history of coastal storm damage, nobody in New Jersey or New York was prepared for the devastation caused by Hurricane Sandy in October 2012. Sandy made landfall in New Jersey near Brigantine accompanied by heavy rains, 80 mph sustained winds with gusts over 90 mph, and a record-breaking storm surge that coincided with a high tide and a full moon. In New York and New Jersey, the storm surge was fourteen feet above the average low tide. Floods filled the streets. The storm swept houses off their foundations and toppled trees and power lines. In Monmouth County, the Atlantic Ocean came over the seawall and met the Shrewsbury River on Ocean Avenue in Sea Bright and Monmouth Beach, inundating the Sea Bright business district and destroying homes and condominiums on the Sandy Hook Peninsula. Rising river water covered ten percent of my hometown of Oceanport and destroyed its Borough Hall.

Hurricane Sandy[4] was the costliest natural disaster in the history of New Jersey[5]. Businesses lost up to $30 billion. Thirty-eight people lost their lives, and 346,000 homes were damaged or destroyed. The storm's high winds and heavy rainfall knocked down or damaged over 113,000 trees, many of which fell onto power lines, leaving about 2.7 million people without power for many days. The power outages adversely affected seventy water systems and eighty sewage systems. High waters sank 1,400 boats.

Hurricane Sandy also severely affected New York City and its suburbs, destroying thousands of homes and approximately 250,000 vehicles. The storm flooded the New York City Subway[6] system and of all the vehicular tunnels entering Manhattan[7] except the Lincoln Tunnel[8]. It damaged the

4. https://en.wikipedia.org/wiki/Hurricane_Sandy

5. https://en.wikipedia.org/wiki/History_of_New_Jersey

6. https://en.wikipedia.org/wiki/New_York_City_Subway

7. https://en.wikipedia.org/wiki/Manhattan

one-hundred-year-old railroad tunnel under the Hudson River between New Jersey and New York. The New York Stock Exchange[9] closed for two consecutive days. Fire destroyed many homes and businesses, including over 100 homes in Breezy Point, Queens[10] because firefighters could not reach them through the flood waters. Large parts of the city and surrounding areas lost electricity[11] for several days. A crane collapse forced evacuation of several thousand people in midtown Manhattan[12] for six days. Power failures closed Bellevue Hospital Center[13] and a few other large hospitals, which had to be evacuated, and disrupted voice and data communication in lower Manhattan[14]. Economic losses in New York City and New York State amounted to $51.8 billion. Tragically, fifty-three people lost their lives.

Another devastating storm hit the Northeast in 2021. Three days after Hurricane Ida [15]made landfall in Louisiana, its weakened remnants tore into the Northeast and claimed at least 43 lives across New York[16], New Jersey[17], and two other states. This storm's onslaught served as an ominous sign of climate change's capacity to wreak havoc. Hurricane Sandy did its damage mostly through tidal surges. Most of Hurricane Ida's toll — both in human life and property damage — reflected the extent to which the sheer volume of rain simply overwhelmed the infrastructure of a region built in and for a different meteorological era.

Pointing to Hurricane Sandy and the severe hurricanes that have hit Florida, Louisiana, and Texas over the last dozen years, experts think the warming oceans and rising sea levels caused by global warming are contributing to

---

8. https://en.wikipedia.org/wiki/Lincoln_Tunnel

9. https://en.wikipedia.org/wiki/New_York_Stock_Exchange

10. https://en.wikipedia.org/wiki/Breezy_Point,_Queens

11. https://en.wikipedia.org/wiki/Power_outage

12. https://en.wikipedia.org/wiki/Midtown_Manhattan

13. https://en.wikipedia.org/wiki/Bellevue_Hospital_Center

14. https://en.wikipedia.org/wiki/Lower_Manhattan

15. https://www.nytimes.com/live/2021/09/03/nyregion/nyc-flooding-storm

16. https://www.nytimes.com/2021/09/03/nyregion/nyc-trains-amtrak-hurricane-ida.html

17. https://www.nytimes.com/2021/09/03/nyregion/new-jersey-ida-deaths.html

making storms more powerful, dangerous, and deadly. They note that the US spends a staggering amount on costs secondary to natural disasters. Between 1980 and 2021, they amounted to over $2 trillion. During that time there were 15,347 disaster related deaths. They conclude that CO2 levels and temperature increases over the past four decades "are strongly positively correlated with the number of and total cost due to billion-dollar disasters." The annual number of billion-dollar disasters in the US will continue to increase. Measures are therefore needed to mitigate those costs. [83]

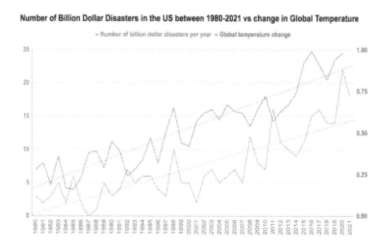

IN 2022, THE WORLD Meteorological Organization (WMO) reported that melting glaciers and ice caps in Greenland and Antarctica, as well as the expansion of the volume of oceans due to heat, have fueled sea level rise. This rise threatens the existence of coastal communities and sometimes entire countries. [84] Over 128 million Americans live in coastal counties, and more than $1 trillion worth of property is within seven hundred feet of the coast. The Environmental Protection Agency reports that forty percent of the US population living in US coastal counties face permanent inundation and flooding threats from sea level rise, intense rains, high tide flooding, and severe storms.[85]

Under these circumstances, state, county, and municipal officials should heed the advice about land use that I presented in 2010 at a National Oceanic and Atmospheric Administration (NOAA) forum. While in Washington with Climate Communities, I moderated a roundtable about building a strong partnership between NOAA and local governments across the country in their work to reduce GHG emissions and prepare for sea level rise resulting from climate change. I pointed out, for example, that with twenty-nine miles of Atlantic Ocean beaches and twenty-eight miles on the shores of Sandy Hook and Raritan Bays, over 400,000 Monmouth County residents faced multi-hazard vulnerability to flooding from coastal storms and higher than usual tides. Panelists from Florida and other states described similar vulnerabilities.

I noted that Monmouth County had implemented a coastal evacuation plan, but that its Coastal Monmouth Region Plan was still relying heavily on shoreline armoring with seawalls, bulkheads, and beach replenishment. I warned that future adaptation to sea level rise would be not just an engineering issue but also a land use issue; therefore, I urged the attendees from coastal states to consider various land use options:

- Minimize development on beach, dune, and coastal wetland retreat zones to minimize the need for structural responses.
- Preserve wetlands that provide flood control, buffer storm surges, and harbor fish nursery areas.
- Use dune protection and stabilization or salt marsh restoration instead of shoreline armoring, such as sea walls.
- Acquire developed properties in high hazard zones as part of a "Coastal Blue Acres" buyout program.
- Identify and map at-risk sensitive habitats and special status species to address changes in habitats or populations.
- "Roll" with shoreline retreat by using sediments and dredged material to elevate wetland boundaries in anticipation of increasing tidal inundation.

County Commissioner Barbara McMorrow retired in 2010. My third term as Monmouth County Commissioner expired in December 2010. This time I lost my bid for re-election by a large margin thanks to the right-wing wave led by Tea Party Republicans. After Commissioner Amy Mallet also lost her bid for re-election in 2011, the GHG Reduction Advisory Committee and its recommendations withered and died. Monmouth County's Master Plan published in 2016 stated that the GHG Reduction Advisory Committee's plan should "be expanded" to include "cost-benefit analyses of each potential proposal." This was a dodge. The benefit of not having the planet rendered uninhabitable by global warming caused by *homo sapiens* will exceed the cost of all potential county initiatives aimed at preventing such a consummation.

The consequences of the 2010 election and the accompanying pivot from traditional print and broadcast media to propagandizing social media, radio, and television were dire not only for Monmouth County but also for the nation and the world. Unlike most Americans, the Tea Party activists who supported Republican candidates that year did not think the Earth was warming. Pro fossil fuel industry groups spent record sums that swept a new crop of climate deniers into Congress. The House of Representatives flipped to the Republicans, who stalled President Obama's climate control agenda for the rest of his presidency.

The damage continued after the 2016 election. Within weeks of taking office in 2017, President Donald Trump began rescinding or weakening a record number of regulations designed to cut emissions, protect wildlife, ban dangerous pesticides, and limit water and air pollution. Denying the overwhelming scientific consensus on the causes of climate change, Trump opened new land to oil and gas drilling and issued permits for controversial oil pipelines. Vowing to "end the war on coal," he dismantled the Obama Administration's plan to reduce carbon emissions from power plants. He pulled the US out of the UN Paris Climate Agreement to lower carbon emissions. The only other countries not signing the agreement were Syria and Nicaragua. Domestically, Trump attempted to undermine the agencies, institutions and core values undergirding environmental protection and climate control.

Last Chance to Save the Planet

Trump's successor, President Joe Biden, and progressive governors like New Jersey Governor Phil Murphy have tried to repair the damage. While impressive, their programs may prove too little too late to halt climate change absent more aggressive international, national, and local efforts. In December 2023 over 200 attendees at the United Nations Climate Change Conference (COP28) agreed on a non-binding "stocktake" that calls on countries to take actions towards achieving, at a global scale, a tripling of renewable energy capacity and doubling energy efficiency improvements by 2030. The list also includes accelerating efforts towards the phase-down of unabated coal power, phasing out inefficient fossil fuel subsidies, and other measures that can drive the transition away from fossil fuels in energy systems, in a just, orderly, and equitable manner, with developed countries continuing to take the lead.[86] Unfortunately, the stocktake lacks tough language on outlawing construction of new coal-burning power plants and specific commitments to help finance poorer nations' energy transitions. Oil production in the United States continues to surge. European countries are spending billions on new terminals to import liquefied natural gas, and countries like China and India are still building large new coal plants to satisfy growing energy demand.

A massive review of ancient atmospheric carbon-dioxide levels and corresponding temperatures lays out a daunting picture of where the Earth's climate may be headed. In the late 1700s, the air contained about 280 parts per million (ppm) of $CO2$. We are now up to 420 ppm, an increase of about 50%; by the end of the century, we could reach 600 ppm or more. As a result, we are already somewhere along an uncertain warming curve, with a rise of about 1.2 degrees C (2.2 degrees F) since the late 19th century.[87]

The Intergovernmental Panel on Climate Change (IPCC) "AR 6 Synthesis Report, Climate Change 2023" warns that climate change is a threat to human well-being and planetary health.[88] If humans continue to burn coal, oil, and natural gas, global greenhouse gas emissions will continue to increase with ongoing contributions from unsustainable energy use, overdevelopment, deforestation, and methane-generating dairy and meat consumption and production.

The IPCC report says that climate change is already causing widespread disruption in every region in the world. Withering droughts, extreme heat, and record floods already threaten food security and the livelihoods of millions of people. Half the global population faces water insecurity at least one month per year. Wildfires are scorching larger areas than ever before, leading to irreversible changes to the landscape in many regions. The New York metropolitan area experienced the worst air pollution in the world in 2023 because of uncontrolled Canadian wildfires. Higher temperatures are also enabling the spread of vector-borne diseases, such as West Nile virus, Lyme disease, and malaria, as well as water-borne diseases like cholera. Climate change is also harming species and entire ecosystems. It could render parts of the earth uninhabitable, prompting refugee flows on an unprecedented scale, destabilizing governments around the world.

The report argues that nations are not doing enough to protect cities, farms, and coastlines from the hazards that climate change has already unleashed, let alone from the even greater disasters in store as the planet keeps heating. Many glaciers around the world will either disappear or lose most of their mass. Arctic and Antarctic Sea ice and ice sheets will melt, and permafrost will thaw. There will be rapid sea level rise, forcing millions to retreat from coastlines. Storms will be stronger, heatwaves and droughts longer, and precipitation more extreme.

The report concludes that there is still one last chance to shift course, but it will require industrialized nations to join immediately to slash greenhouse gases in half by 2030 and then stop adding carbon dioxide to the atmosphere altogether by the early 2050s. Changing course will require immediate, ambitious, and concerted efforts by nations, states, counties, and municipalities to slash emissions, build resilience, and conserve ecosystems.

An array of strategies is available for reducing greenhouse gas emissions, such as scaling up wind and solar power, shifting to electric vehicles and electric heat pumps in buildings, curbing methane emissions from oil and gas operations, and protecting forests. A shift away from the consumption of meat is another critical path. Cattle generate significant global warming methane emissions and are defoliating native plants and vegetation. Unfortunately, changing the bovine diet of wealthy humans will not be easy. There are, however, ways to change food and forestry production systems and manage land conservation to mitigate climate change while increasing sustainability, improving rural incomes, and easing adaptation to a warming world. [89]

Scientists and engineers are developing technological solutions. Some propose aerosol injection of sulfur dioxide into the stratosphere to generate highly reflective particles that bounce back a fraction of the sunlight hitting the atmosphere. Others believe that spraying salt water right above the ocean would create small cloud droplets, resulting in brighter low-lying clouds that would reflect sunlight before it warms the planet. Another scheme involves injecting particles into the troposphere to thin out wispy cirrus clouds that warm the planet by trapping infrared radiation. Opponents view these techniques as a moral hazard, fearing that geoengineering will encourage polluters to keep polluting instead of doing the arduous work of cutting planet-warming gases such as carbon dioxide and methane. They are also concerned about unintended consequences. Inconsistent cooling could change precipitation patterns affecting food and water security. Stratospheric aerosol injection could disrupt Asian and African summer monsoons crucial for agriculture. Sulfur particles could cause air pollution, increase acid rain, and even turn the sky white. Relying on theoretical technologies is risky and could expose us to a unique set of devastating hazards.[90]

A different group of scientists and entrepreneurs is embarking on ambitious—and sometimes controversial—projects to remove carbon dioxide from ambient air and lock it away. These include direct air capture, mineralizing carbon and oceans, electrifying seas, farming underwater, and fertilizing oceans. What these efforts have in common is that to their many detractors, the very idea of sucking carbon out of the air is a diversion from the far more urgent task of radically cutting carbon dioxide emissions to begin with. Many scientists maintain, however, that any realistic pathway to dealing with the climate emergency projected by the IPCC must include carbon removal on a vast scale. [91]

Regardless of what approach they take, countries, provinces, states, counties, and municipalities will have to spend vast amounts of money on GHG reduction, adaptation, and remediation of loss and damage to prevent further destruction of our earthly home. For countries to meet national energy and climate goals on time and in full, wind and solar energy will have to account for over 80% of the total increase in global power capacity in the next two decades, compared with less than 40% over the past two decades. In the International Energy Agency's Net Zero Emissions by 2050 Scenario, wind and solar will have to account for almost 90% of the increase. Because electrical grids are essential to decarbonize electricity supply and effectively integrate renewables, reaching national energy and climate goals will require the addition and refurbishment of over eighty million kilometers of grids by 2040. That is the equivalent of the entire existing global grid. The acceleration of renewable energy deployment will also require construction of new transmission corridors to connect renewable resources—such as solar projects in the desert and offshore wind turbines—to distant demand centers like cities and industrial areas. [92]

America rejoined the Paris Accord after the election of President Joseph Biden in 2020. The Inflation Reduction Act, signed by President Biden in 2022, represents the single-largest investment in climate action in American history. The government allocated $370 billion to clean energy, energy security, and environmental justice. It offered businesses and consumers subsidies and tax credits to adopt green technologies, putting the United States on a path to reduce carbon emissions by forty percent by 2030. The Inflation Reduction Act includes provisions inserted by New Jersey Congressman Frank Pallone that clarify and reinforce the authority of the Environmental Protection Agency (EPA) to regulate greenhouse gas emissions as air pollutants in response to the Supreme Court's decision in *West Virginia v. EPA* [93] that limited the EPA's authority under the Clean Air Act.

The question that remains, however, is whether the Inflation Reduction Act and worldwide climate mitigation efforts will suffice? Many Republican federal and state legislators want the United States to continue to burn fossil fuels. Dozens of conservative groups organized by the Heritage Foundation have issued a policy playbook that would shred regulations designed to curb greenhouse gases, dismantle every federal clean energy program, and boost fossil fuel production. Federal, state, and local regulations and byzantine permitting requirements delay wind and solar energy projects. Fossil fuel interests support and fund local "not in my backyard" (NIMBY) protest groups seeking to block them, and right-wing plaintiffs file lawsuits seeking to overturn approvals. Citizens favoring climate mitigation efforts must counteract political obstruction and force state, county, and municipal governments to expedite the approval process for clean energy projects. [94]

The last chance to save the planet may rest in the hands of Millennials and Generations Z and Alpha. New Jersey is the first state in the union to recognize this by requiring public schools to teach students about climate change as early as kindergarten, and throughout their classes, even in physical education. The climate change aspects of the New Jersey Student Learning Standards help students understand how and why climate change happens, apprehend the impact it has on our local and global communities, and act in informed and sustainable ways.[95] Other state, county, and municipal school districts would be well-advised to follow New Jersey's lead.

Another major step that states can take is to amend their constitutions to add a Green Amendment providing that every person has an inalienable right on a par with the rights to free speech and freedom of religion, to a clean and healthy environment. It should guarantee citizens clean water, clean air, a stable climate, and ecologically healthy habitats. In 2020, sixteen young Montana residents, then aged two through eighteen, sued alleging that the state government's pro-fossil fuel policies contributing to climate change violated the Montana constitution. In 2023, the judge in *Held v. State of Montana*[96] ruled the policies violated constitutional mandate that the "state and each person shall maintain and improve a clean and healthful environment in Montana for present and future generations." The lawsuit overturned a provision in the Montana Environmental Policy Act which the legislature amended to prevent environmental reviews from considering "regional, national or global" environmental impacts—a provision the complaint called the "climate change exception." In states whose constitutions include the Green

Amendment, the decision of the United States Supreme Court in *Moore v. Harper* rejecting the "independent state legislature" theory should enhance the prospects for the success of lawsuits of this type. The Supreme Court ruled that when legislatures make laws, they are bound by the very documents that give them life.[97] While *Moore* holds state courts must ensure that laws for federal elections comply with their state constitutions, this legal principle should apply as well to such federal laws as the Clean Air Act and the Clean Water Act.

Failure to heed the warnings in the IPCC Reports and take meaningful action internationally, nationally, and in states, counties and municipalities will bring about the consequences predicted by Apostle Peter 2,000 years ago: "The day of the Lord will come as a thief in the night, in which the heavens will pass away with a great noise, and the elements will melt with fervent heat; both the earth and the works that are in it will be burned up." 2 Peter 3:10

Chapter 10: Defending the Waters of the Earth

———

The poor and needy seek water, but there is none, their tongues fail for thirst, I the Lord, will hear them; ... I will open the rivers in desolate heights, and fountains in the midst of the valleys; I will make the wilderness a pool of water, and the dry land springs of water.——Isaiah 41:18

I was born on the "Jersey Shore" in Long Branch, New Jersey. My parents used to take me for walks on its boardwalk to breathe the ocean air, eat ice cream, and play at the amusements lining its pier. We would go to Sea Bright beach in the summer to swim and build sandcastles. We would also go fishing and crabbing on the Navesink and Shrewsbury rivers. Life in and on the water was always an important part of my life. That is why I focused on environmental issues related to water quality when I held public office. The attempted murder of the planet described in the last chapter is both a terrestrial and aquatic threat to the wellbeing of humankind. It is urgent that we defend the waters of the earth.

The United Nations Educational, Scientific and Cultural Organization. (UNESCO) reports that water use has been increasing globally by 1% per year over the last forty years and will grow at a similar rate through to 2050, driven by a combination of population growth, socio-economic development, and changing consumption patterns. Water scarcity is becoming endemic because of the local impact of physical water stress, and freshwater pollution is speeding up and spreading. Because of climate change, seasonal water scarcity will increase in regions where it is currently abundant and worsen in regions where water is already in short supply. [98]

Access to sufficient, safe, and accessible drinking water is not just a developing world issue. Too many Americans face water insecurity because of groundwater exhaustion, infrastructure challenges, climate change conditions and contamination, with devastating effects on public health and community prosperity.[99] Particularly concerning is that global warming is severely depleting aquifers that supply ninety percent of the nation's water systems. They transformed vast stretches of America into some of the world's most bountiful farmland, but their decline threatens irreversible harm to the American economy and society. [100] To address water scarcity, county, state, and national governments need to promote water conservation, reduce water demand, control development in water-scarce regions, and mitigate climate change. [101]

During my first two terms as a Monmouth County Commissioner, I drew attention to the fact that rapid development and the accompanying increase in population were outstripping the county's capacity to supply fresh water to its residents. In the northern portions of the county, underground aquifers were being depleted and threatened with the intrusion of salt water. The County Commissioners worked proactively with the New Jersey Water Supply Authority to ease this problem by constructing the Manasquan River Reservoir. It came online in 1990, but Monmouth County and New Jersey remain vulnerable to dry spells and drought in the summer months, requiring water conservation and restrictions.

The County Commissioners also took action to preserve water quality. In 1984, developers sought approval from the Monmouth County Planning Board for a proposed development on the Marlu-Twitchell farm that would have included 470 housing units, a golf course, and a clubhouse/banquet facility on the banks of the Swimming River Reservoir. The development would have used septic tanks that threatened to contaminate the potable water supply for 238,000 county residents. At my request, the county Planning Board studied the Swimming River and Manasquan River watersheds in Monmouth County. It concluded that preservation of open space in these areas was critical to protect the quality of drinking water throughout the county. The Board of County Commissioners responded by acquiring the 457-acre Marlu-Twitchell farm. It also purchased the Dorbrook farm on the opposite bank of the reservoir. An October 8, 1985, Asbury Park Press editorial observed that "the recent purchase of the 388-acre farm by the Monmouth County Board of Freeholders will go far in preserving the character of an area where open space remains the rule, not the exception. It will also ensure that this large parcel of land bordering the Swimming River Reservoir will continue to act as a buffer to protect the water quality of the reservoir."

States and counties throughout the nation must recognize the importance of this type of land conservation and act to preserve open space buffers that protect drinking water. As noted by the United States Environmental Protection Agency (EPA), protecting source water can reduce health risks by preventing exposure to contaminated water. Water utilities meeting the definition of "public water systems" must comply with the requirements of EPA and state drinking water programs under the Safe Drinking Water Act. Protecting source water from contamination helps reduce treatment costs and can reduce the need for complex treatment. Additional benefits associated with source water protection include protecting water quality for wildlife and recreational use and ensuring the availability of adequate water supplies. [102]

After completing my third term as Monmouth County Commissioner in 2010, I assumed a different role in the defense of the waters of the earth by joining the Board of Trustees of the NY/NJ Baykeeper in 2011. I became Chair of the Board in 2015. Chief Executive Officer and Baykeeper Greg Remaud, Baykeeper attorney Michele Langa and an excellent staff are ably advancing Baykeeper's mission to protect, preserve, and restore the Hudson-Raritan Estuary.

An estuary is an area where freshwater rivers and streams meet the ocean and the salty ocean water mixes with the fresh water, resulting in brackish water that is less salty than the ocean. Water continually circulates into and out of an estuary. Tides create the largest flow of saltwater, while rivers produce the largest flow of freshwater. Estuaries are among the most productive and diverse natural systems on earth. The salt and freshwater mix provides a rich environment with high productivity and biodiversity, like coral reefs and rainforests.

The Hudson-Raritan Estuary cuts into the nation's most densely populated metropolitan region. It is a 20-mile indent with eight hundred miles of shoreline that swings counterclockwise from the western tip of Long Island and sweeps past New York City. It continues to New Jersey's urban coast, where the Hudson, Hackensack, Passaic, Rahway, and Raritan rivers meet the Bay. At the southern end is the needle-thin peninsula of Sandy Hook, New Jersey.

The NY-NJ Harbor Estuary is a living web of uplands, biologically rich fresh and saltwater wetlands, beaches, straits, and broad bays. It teems with over two hundred distinct species of fish and over three hundred bird species, including vast schools of migrating shad and herring and flocks of songbirds and raptors. It nourishes urban citizens who seek recreation and rejuvenation in nature. The harbor is the most urban in the world, characterized by a mixture of glass towers, superhighways, and refineries. It is a region teeming with wildlife, yet in need of ecological repair.

When European explorers arrived in the NY-NJ Harbor Estuary, they encountered an astonishing natural abundance of marine animals. Henry Hudson reported "many salmons and mullets, of a foot and a half a piece, and a ray as great as four men could hale into the ship." Oyster beds extended from the mouth of the Raritan River to Yonkers. Each spring a great migration of giant sturgeon, shad, and schools of herring moved through the Estuary and up its tributaries to spawn. New York City was the place to eat oysters! As New York grew as a city, so did the consumption of this popular mollusk.

The NY-NJ Harbor Estuary has suffered from pollution and habitat destruction over the last three centuries. Oysters and clams became contaminated, fish suffocated or left for lack of oxygen, and people stopped swimming in the water. In 1924-25, typhoid fever caused by polluted oysters killed 150 people in New York, Chicago, and Washington, DC. It was the deadliest outbreak of food-borne illness in US history. During the twentieth century, development gradually overtook the natural areas on which fish, wildlife and birds depended. It destroyed or altered most of the Estuary's shoreline, wetlands, and tributaries. Sand mining, dredging, and dumping disturbed much of its bottom habitat. Fish, shellfish, birds, and wildlife lost areas critical for reproduction, feeding, and growth, reducing these habitat areas to the bare minimum needed to sustain life in the Estuary.

Water quality reached its lowest point in the 1960s. With the construction of sewage treatment facilities and reduced industrial pollution, the Estuary's waters began a slow improvement. Habitat, however, has not fully recovered. Although the rate of habitat loss, particularly in the wetlands, has declined somewhat because of the Clean Water Act of 1972, areas already lost to development are not recovering on their own. Unlike water pollution, most habitat loss is permanent. Salt marsh cannot push through pavement, and oysters cannot settle on muddied beds. Oysters are functionally extinct in the Hudson-Raritan Estuary.

Andrew Willner had just started a small boat building and repair yard on Staten Island, New York. When his daughter, then 10 years old, visited the yard and was upset because she could not go swimming because of pollution, Willner got furious. He sought advice from the Riverkeeper on the Hudson River, the Soundkeeper in Long Island, and Baykeepers in Delaware and San Francisco. With their help, he launched the New York /New Jersey Baykeeper program in 1989. He used the power of advocacy and the law to combat water pollution and safeguard the Hudson-Raritan Estuary. The water was much cleaner when he retired in 2008, and his non-profit organization had grown in strength and influence. [103]

NY/NJ Baykeeper pioneered oyster restoration in New Jersey's portion of Raritan Bay and created the first living shoreline there. Oysters provide multiple benefits, including protecting the coastline against erosion, serving as speed bumps for waves during storms, acting as natural water filters, and creating habitat for marine life. A single oyster can clean up to fifty gallons of water a day. Oyster reefs help protect the coastline, an important aim because of the sea level rise resulting from climate change. Baykeeper cultivated juvenile oysters at an Aquaculture Facility at Naval Weapons Station Earle (NWSE) facility in Leonardo, New Jersey and released them onto Baykeeper's oyster reefs in Raritan Bay. Baykeeper's Restoration Team monitored them for survivorship and growth, tested water quality, and studied biodiversity around the reef.

Shoreline erosion is a natural process that is threatening NJ's coastal resiliency. In 2016, Baykeeper and the Rutgers University Center for Urban Environmental Sustainability (CUES) installed a 0.91 acre Living Shoreline next to Ware Creek at NWSE. Oysters set on vertical oyster reef structures, or castles, can reduce storm energies and soil erosion. In 2017, Baykeeper found its oysters were naturally reproducing and creating a healthy habitat on this reef for the first time. Building on the success of Baykeeper's program, the Inflation Reduction Act included $2.6 billion to conserve and restore coastal habitats and protect coastal communities modeled on Congressman Pallone's living shorelines legislation[1]. Living shoreline infrastructure projects use natural materials and systems such as dunes, wetlands, and oyster reefs to support the natural flood resilience of healthy shoreline ecosystems. Natural infrastructure is cost-effective and adaptable to changing environmental conditions. It also enhances ecosystem functions, which can improve water quality and wildlife habitat protection.

Monmouth University's Urban Coast Institute is expanding Baykeeper's program at NWSE. [104] Baykeeper continues to manage a 1-acre oyster reef at Soundview Park in the Bronx River, New York. It provides substrate for new oysters to attach to, increases habitat in the area, and encourages natural recruitment for a self-sustaining reef. The "Scientific Reef" portion provides space for scientific experiments. The "Community Reef" is a small sub-plot within the large reef, providing a unique opportunity for eco-volunteerism in the NYC metro area. Volunteers get into the water and observe oyster biology and ecology up close, monitoring survivorship, growth, and biodiversity. Another major program operated by the Billion Oyster Project, a New York City-based nonprofit organization, is attempting to engage people in the effort to restore oysters to New York Harbor. [105]

The NY-NJ Harbor Estuary Region is home to twenty million people and hundreds of species of birds, fish, and other wildlife. Preserving natural habitat is essential in this heavily developed region because open space protects water supplies, improves water quality, buffers flood-prone areas, and creates and

---

1. http://pallone.house.gov/media/press-releases/pallone-murphy-announce-introduction-bill-help-coastal-communities-combat

improves parks. Since 1989, Baykeeper and its partners have preserved and restored over three thousand acres of critical habitat amid one of the most densely populated and industrialized ports in the nation. Baykeeper is collaborating with the Friends of the Liberty State Park in Jersey City to protect and restore a priceless American urban oasis in the middle of densely populated metropolitan northern New Jersey. Called "New Jersey's Central Park," Liberty State Park has something Central Park does not: spectacular views of the Statue of Liberty, Ellis Island, the Manhattan skyline, New York Harbor, and the Verrazano Narrows Bridge. With over five million annual visitors, it is New Jersey's most popular park. It encompasses approximately six hundred acres of land and six hundred acres of water, and contains significant natural, historic, recreational, scenic, and cultural resources. [106]

Baykeeper is using the power of legal actions and advocacy campaigns to protect, preserve and restore waterways, wetlands, and habitats throughout the Estuary. Its legal advocacy concentrates on "heritage pollutants" such as contaminated sediments and works to make sure private companies, state agencies, and municipalities comply with stormwater regulations. Baykeeper investigates facilities that pose a threat to human health and the environment and files lawsuits to hold polluters accountable for restoring polluted resources to their prior condition.

Point and Non-point Water Pollution

A major aspect of Baykeeper's work is to reduce both point and non-point water pollution. Fifty years following passage of the federal Clean Water Act, most US water bodies still do not meet water quality standards. They are neither fishable nor swimmable. The Clean Water Act has helped control point source pollution, including effluent from industrial sources with the construction of wastewater treatment plants, but discharges from sewage and septic systems still contribute a substantial amount to nutrient pollution. The EPA considers this one of America's most widespread, costly, and challenging environmental problems.

Today, only about 62 percent of urban dwellers worldwide have access to sewers. They mostly live in high and upper-middle-income countries. In low-income countries, sewer coverage has dropped from about 24 percent to about 17 percent in recent years because of urban population growth. Many cities are so dense and growing so quickly that it is impossible to install more conventional underground sewers. We urgently need other options. [107]

The Clean Water Act has curtailed but not eliminated point and non-point source pollution. Non-point pollution includes runoff of oil, pet waste, pesticide, herbicide, fertilizer, road salt, bacteria, sediment, and other contaminants from impervious surfaces, such as roads and parking lots. Regulating non-point pollution is the responsibility of the states. Only a few of them have implemented and enforced robust controls over non-point sources. As a result, non-point source pollution remains the leading cause of water quality problems in the United States today.[108]

APPROXIMATELY 772 CITIES in the US rely on combined sewer and stormwater outflow pipes (CSOs) like the one shown above to carry storm water, domestic sewage, and industrial waste to sewage treatment facilities. They are a major source of water pollution. This antiquated infrastructure is common in older urban areas. In northern New Jersey for example, whenever it rains a twentieth of an inch or more, the combined outflow of raw sewage and stormwater runoff overwhelms sewage treatment plants, resulting in the release of human and animal waste, oil, pesticides, toxic contaminants, and floatable materials such as syringes and tampons into rivers, bays, and the ocean. CSOs discharge upwards of twenty-three billion gallons of this toxic brew annually into New Jersey's coastal waters. Loaded with pathogens, it can cause respiratory, ear, and eye infections and diseases, such as gastroenteritis, hepatitis, and dysentery. The wastewater also threatens drinking water supplies, impairs the viability of aquatic habitats, and kills fish. For more than a century, this major flaw in New Jersey's wastewater infrastructure has caused serious pollution in river, bay, and ocean water in the Hudson/Raritan Estuary from New York City to Sandy Hook. As a result, authorities have banned swimming, fishing, and shellfish harvesting in the affected waters. I call it the "CSO curse."

Congress enacted the Clean Water Act of 1972 to restore and maintain clean and healthy water. It amended the law in 1977 to regulate the municipal and industrial discharge of untreated wastewater into rivers, lakes, and coastal waters. During my year in the New Jersey State Senate, I sponsored a $50 million Bond Act for Stormwater Management and Sewer Overflow Abatement to help New Jersey meet this requirement. Approved by the voters in 1989, it provided grants and low-interest loans to local governments to offset the costs of stormwater and CSO capital projects. New Jersey DEP did not use the money to comply with the 1994 EPA policy on Combined Sewer Overflows, and New Jersey fell far behind other states.

In 2013, NY/NJ Baykeeper and Hackensack Riverkeeper sued the DEP to force it to upgrade its CSO regulatory program. The DEP responded in 2015 by imposing stricter permit requirements on sewer authorities, but there has been little progress. At Baykeeper's urging, many authorities, municipalities and community groups have adopted "Green Infrastructure" technologies such as rain barrels, cisterns, rain gardens, green roofs, bioretention basins, vegetated swales, and permeable pavements. They allow rainfall to infiltrate into the soil and recharge aquifers. By stopping stormwater from reaching sewers, they curtail non-point pollution runoff into streams, rivers, and bays. A major green infrastructure project supported and funded by the Victoria Foundation through Baykeeper is Newark Doing Infrastructure Green (DIG). DIG uses green infrastructure as the first line of defense to better manage stormwater runoff, improve water quality, build resiliency to flooding, and reduce combined sewer overflows (CSOs). It will have a positive impact on water quality in the Passaic River and its tributaries. We urgently need more efforts of this type in large cities in the United States and abroad.

While helpful, however, these approaches fall short of what we need to prevent CSOs from overflowing when storms and heavy rains cause higher than normal runoff and urban flooding. In January 2021, Baykeeper told the DEP that the plans submitted by sewer treatment permit holders to eliminate CSOs over twenty to forty years were unsatisfactory. There are several reasons for this unacceptable deferral of the "CSO curse" to the next generation. First, the fix will require large capital projects involving traditional and advanced engineering. Known as "Gray Infrastructure," these include sewer/storm drain separation, satellite holding and/or treatment facilities, sewer plant expansion, non-point pollution controls, and "end of pipe" netting, screens, and treatment. Second, these fixes are extremely expensive. CSO correction just in New Jersey was estimated in 2014 to cost $9.3 billion; decentralized wastewater treatment, $2.2 billion; repair and improvement of secondary and advanced treatment, $6.3 billion; and non-point pollution control, $1.8 billion. The price tag is higher today. Third, most of the 217 CSO outfall pipes in the state belong to twenty communities and eight sewage treatment authorities in older cities and counties. These areas have a higher percentage of poor and low-income residents. Their governments have enormous financial challenges. Besides CSO remediation, they must address deferred maintenance of existing wastewater treatment facilities and improve other public services.

The CSO problem will get worse. The Intergovernmental Panel on Climate Change predicts that greenhouse gas emissions from human activities will increase global warming throughout the 21st century, causing more intense rainfall and associated flooding as well as continued sea level rise in coastal areas. In 2012, Hurricane Sandy provided a preview of how these changes will aggravate the "CSO curse." The storm overwhelmed waste-water treatment plants and sent over ten billion gallons of raw and partly treated sewage into streets, rivers, canals, and bays.

In 2021, the US Congress passed the Infrastructure Investment and Jobs Act. It provided $280 million each year for Overflow and Stormwater Grants program over five years ($1.4 billion in total) and $14.6 billion as part of the Sewer Overflow and Stormwater Re-use Municipal Grants program. These appropriations, for which there will be national competition, will fall far short of what New Jersey and states, counties, and municipalities throughout the country need to upgrade wastewater treatment infrastructure. There must be more federal and state funding so that sewer treatment authorities can address CSO remediation in a manner that acknowledges the urgency of the situation and ends the "CSO curse."

The Plastic Scourge

Monmouth County was struggling to comply with the state requirement that the county dispose of its own solid waste when I was a County Commissioner, but county and state recycling mandates did not cover plastics. In 1987, I proposed amending Monmouth County's solid waste management plan to require a 15-cent deposit on all plastic beverage containers. Its intent was to encourage retailers and bottling companies to use glass and aluminium beverage containers and to put pressure on the manufacturing sector to develop recyclable plastic containers. The ordinance would have required retailers to accept and pay a 15-cent deposit on clear, undamaged empty plastic beverage containers of the type they sell. Every distributer would be required to pay retailers the refund value plus a cent-and-a-half handling charge.

I argued that the plastic bottle deposit ordinance would help ease the problem of discarded plastic containers on land and at sea that was plaguing Monmouth County. At the hearing on the proposed ordinance, Valerie Maxwell of Clean Ocean Action said that in less than an hour on one day, volunteers plucked 94 bags of plastic containers from county beaches. Jack Charlton of Monmouth County Friends of Clearwater noted the durability of plastics: "Our great-great-great-great-great-great-great-grandchildren could trip over a plastic bottle carelessly discarded today."

The New Jersey Food Council and representatives from bottlers, including Coke and 7-Up, opposed the proposed ordinance. Some attendees at the hearing wore orange stickers that said, "NO Bottle Bill." Pepsi-Cola Bottling Co. threatened to sue to block the ordinance. A Register editorial on Monmouth's bottle bill said, "We applaud D'Amico for devising an ambitious bottle deposit ordinance which may become a New Jersey model." Unfortunately, the Republican majority on the Board of County Commissioners withdrew its support for it.

Global plastic production and use has grown exponentially since the 1950s, with around nine million people employed globally in polymer production and plastic processing industries. The growth has occurred because fossil fuel companies are using ethane from natural gas fracking to make plastics, which is cheaper than using oil. Currently, the world produces 430 million metric tons of plastics each year, of which over two-thirds are short-lived products which soon become waste. Plastic production will triple by 2060 if 'business-as-usual' continues. [109]

IN 2015, NY/NJ BAYKEEPER researcher Sandra Meola Bodner conducted a first-of-its-kind study of plastic pollution in the waterways of New York City and northern New Jersey. It turned up the sobering statistic that about

165 million plastic particles were floating in the estuary, stretching from the Mario Cuomo Bridge, down to the lower Hudson River, and south to Sandy Hook Bay in New Jersey. That is over 256,000 particles per square kilometer. Eighty-five percent of the particles counted were "microplastics," five millimeters, about the size of a grain of rice, or smaller. Microplastics mimic plankton, an important food source for fish and seabirds, and they also absorb toxins commonly found in polluted waters, like PCBs, pesticides, and flame retardants.

Researchers have found microplastics (MPs) and nano plastics (NPs) in the deepest recesses of the ocean, in pristine mountain glaciers, in breast milk, and in human bodies. They are also a major ecotoxicological concern for aquatic animals. However, comprehensive knowledge about the exposure routes and toxic effects of MPs and NPs on animals and human health is lacking. Current scientific literature highlights ingestion, inhalation, and dermal contacts as major exposure routes. Serious health effects suspected and requiring further investigation include oxidative stress[2], cytotoxicity, DNA damage, inflammation, immune response, neurotoxicity[3], and metabolic disruption. There are also adverse effects on digestive systems, immunology, respiratory systems, reproductive systems, and nervous systems. [110]

Author Mark O'Connell summed up the situation in his opinion piece for the New York Times:

> There is plastic in our bodies; it's in our lungs and in our bowels and in the blood that pulses through us. We can't see it, and we can't feel it, but it is there. It is there in the water we drink and the food we eat, and even in the air we breathe. We don't know, yet, what it's doing to us, because we have only quite recently become aware of its presence; but since we have learned of it, it has become a source of profound and multifarious cultural anxiety.... Maybe this has been our fate all along, to achieve communion with our own garbage.... When we look at the decomposing bodies of those trash-filled birds,

---

2. https://www.sciencedirect.com/topics/agricultural-and-biological-sciences/oxidative-stress

3. https://www.sciencedirect.com/topics/agricultural-and-biological-sciences/neurotoxicity

we know that we are looking not just at what we are doing to the world, but also what our damaged world is doing to us. [111]

For more than a decade, scientists have warned that humankind is leaving so much plastic in the natural environment that future archaeologists will mark this era by the synthetic waste that was left behind—in short, the Plastic Age. The Pew Trusts report "Confronting Ocean Plastic Pollution" states that this is especially true in the ocean, where people dump about eleven million metric tons of plastic each year. Plastics in the ocean come in myriad familiar forms, from shopping bags and takeout food containers to water bottles, toothbrushes, toys, bubble wrap, household appliances, and much more. Plastic litters every coastline on the planet and throughout the seas, including the deepest and most remote regions. To prevent the dumping of plastic from nearly tripling by 2040, we need to take urgent, large-scale action. [112]

Plastic is indestructible and non-biodegradable. Manufacturers produce, sell, and consumers use ninety-five percent of plastic packaging as one-and-done products like condiment packets, food wrapping, and bubble wrap. These products end up in the trash as they have little chance of being recycled. Only nine percent of plastic waste gets recycled globally. The Pew Trusts report that breaking the "plastic wave" will require "immediate, ambitious, and concerted actions" such as reducing plastic production, substituting paper and compostable materials, designing products and packaging for recycling, expanding waste collection rates in middle- and low-income countries, increasing mechanical recycling, developing plastic-to-plastic chemical recycling, building facilities that don't allow plastic to leak out, and reducing plastic waste exports.

The UN Intergovernmental Negotiating committee on Plastic Pollution is developing the first international, legally binding treaty on plastic pollution on land and at sea. [113] It envisions a systems-change scenario that combines reducing the most problematic and unnecessary plastic uses with a transformation towards circularity in plastics by accelerating three key market shifts: (1) reuse, (2) recycle, and (3) reorient and diversify the market for sustainable and safe plastic alternatives. [114] Participating countries are divided into two camps. Norway and Rwanda are leading a coalition that wants to end plastic pollution by 2040 by cutting production and limiting some chemicals used in making plastics. Saudi Arabia is leading a group of countries that have large petroleum industries and prefer to focus on recycling and waste management.

The fossil fuel industry, which is facing public policies subsidizing renewable energy and electric vehicles, will not readily abandon its $523 billion plastic profit center expected to reach a value of more than $810 billion by 2030. [115] It is therefore advocating a process called chemical or advanced recycling. It uses heat to break down plastics into liquid and gas to produce an oil-like mixture or basic chemicals. Industry leaders say that they can make that mixture back into plastic pellets to produce new products. Beyond Plastics and International Pollutants Elimination Network (IPEN) have issued a report saying this technology has not worked for decades, is still failing, and threatens the environment, the climate, human health, and environmental justice. [116]

Communities around the world are banning plastic shopping bags, and restaurants are forgoing plastic straws. The European Parliament has proposed a ban, from 2030, of single-use plastic packaging items for fruits and vegetables, condiments in fast food restaurants, thin plastic bags for groceries, and mini cosmetics bottles in hotels. Countries would also be required to ensure that at least 90% of single-use plastic bottles and cans are collected each year from 2029, through deposit return systems. Drinks distributers must ensure 10% of their products are in reusable packaging, although wine is exempted. Takeout food outlets will be required to give customers the option of bringing their own reusable coffee cups or food containers.[117]

These efforts will be helpful but inadequate, as are the piecemeal efforts by some states to curtail plastic waste. Only ten states have adopted bottle deposit laws. Only four states have passed laws like California's Plastic Pollution Prevention and Packaging Producer Responsibility Act (Senate Bill 54), which requires certain types of packaging to be recyclable or compostable by 2032. Its aim is to cut plastic packaging by twenty-five percent in ten years and require sixty-five percent of all single-use plastic packaging to be recycled in the same period. Unfortunately, even recycling has a downside. A study from the University of Strathclyde in Glasgow suggests that thirteen percent of the plastic processed at a state-of-the-art recycling facility in the U.K. ended up as microplastics in the wastewater and the surrounding air. The plant installed a water filtration system that reduced the concentration of microplastics to six percent, or about seventy-five billion particles per cubic meter,[118] but most recycling facilities do not use such a filter.

The bottom line is that we do not need plastics. Only a total ban on the manufacture of non-biodegradable and non-recyclable disposable plastic products will solve the worldwide problem of plastic waste and pollution.[119]

Overfishing

During my brief term in the New Jersey State Senate, I sponsored a bill ensuring that the state complied with federal regulations and limits on the number and size of striped bass that people could take from New Jersey waters. This restriction avoided a total ban on such fishing. The law allowed striped bass to mature so that they would be large and abundant for many years to come. Conservation measures are essential as demand for fish continues to increase around the world.

Fish ranks as one of the most highly traded food commodities and fuels a $362 billion global industry. Half of the world's population relies on fish as a major source of protein. When fish disappear, so do jobs and coastal economies. High demand for seafood is driving overexploitation and environmental degradation. The number of over-fished stocks has tripled globally in half a century. The Food and Agriculture Organization of the United Nations reports that currently, one-third of the world's assessed fisheries are being pushed beyond their biological limits because of high demand for seafood.[120]

Experts recommend aquaculture as an option to cope with the world food demand, but critics accuse it of destroying ecosystems such as mangrove forests and producing polluting effluents. Overfeeding and overfertilization is causing the eutrophication of waters near fish farms. Cultured fish digest only twenty to fifty percent of the nitrogen fed to them. Overfeeding and overfertilization cause the excess nitrogen to flow into adjacent water or get incorporated into sediment. This excess nitrogen leads to phytoplankton blooms, red tides, and the spread of pathogens that produce undesirable odors and kill benthic organisms. Exotic aquacultural species are contaminating and displacing native populations. Monitoring studies have detected a wide range of pharmaceuticals, including hormones, steroids, antibiotics, and parasiticides in soils, surface waters, and groundwaters near fish farms. Fishers who work in these areas argue that this contamination has decreased the population and their catch of wild fish. Aquaculture's dependence on fishmeal and fish oil is causing fish and shellfish to contain dangerous levels of toxins and heavy metals, which should concern consumers. [121]

The potential benefits of aquaculture such as massive food production and economical profits have led the scientific community to seek diverse strategies to minimize the negative impacts. They stress the need to evaluate how much aquaculture bodies of water can sustain and how much effluent they can absorb without disturbing their ecological equilibrium. They advise it is always better to select native instead of exotic species. Other helpful strategies include maintaining a sustainable stocking density, improving feed and feeding strategies, using feeding trays, and increasing feeding frequency. Ways to reduce harm to the environment from waste include using settling lagoons, septic tanks, and recirculation systems, as well as bioremediation and mangrove forests. Poly culture or integrated aquaculture systems can help. To achieve a sustainable aquaculture, environmental agencies must support these strategies worldwide. There also is an urgent need to improve legislation and regulation of aquaculture to ensure its sustainability. [122]

The United States ranks only 18th in the world for aquaculture production. We import up to 90% of the seafood we eat. A sizable portion of the seafood we consume comes from regions where commercial aquaculture practices pose a threat to marine ecosystems, endangered species, and traditional fishing communities. There are currently no comprehensive laws to guide the growth of a substantial aquaculture industry in the US. Congresspeople from both parties have reintroduced the Science-based Equitable Aquaculture Food

(SEAfood) Act that would lay the groundwork for an equitable and inclusive seafood economy of both farmed and wild-caught fish while prioritizing data and science in the development of offshore aquaculture in the US. It needs our support. [123]

To protect and restore wild fish, Earth.org has proposed various solutions to overfishing. With rights-based fishery management, individuals and companies may fish in a certain spot at a certain time. To get a certain share of the catch, they must obey fishing limits or seasons. Catch-share programs[4] give out harvest allowances to individuals or companies to incentivize smarter and timelier fishing instead of a race to catch as much as possible. They also promote a healthy balance between the needs of people, the ocean, and the economy and can guarantee healthier fish populations. Other helpful measures include regulation of fishing nets to reduce the by-catching of unwanted marine species, protection of essential predator species such as sharks and tuna, and enlargement of marine protected areas. Traceability standards can ensure compliance with fishery regulations. Food safety and certification requirements are also essential. [124]

Unfortunately, two-thirds of the world's oceans lie outside national boundaries on the high seas. On March 3, 2023, however, the United Nations forged a long-awaited treaty to safeguard the world's marine biodiversity. When ratified by sixty nations, the Intergovernmental Conference on Marine Biodiversity of Areas Beyond National Jurisdiction treaty will allow countries to designate international waters as protected areas for marine life to preserve species from overfishing, shipping traffic, and plastic pollution. Oil drilling and deep-see mining bans, conservation, sustainable use of marine biodiversity, benefit-sharing of marine genetic resources, environmental impact assessments, and transfer of marine technology will be part of an overall effort to meet the UN Biodiversity Conference's pledge to protect thirty percent of the planet's oceans. [125]

The people using the Earth's waters today are stewards of God's creation. Governments at all levels in the United States and worldwide must protect,

---

4. https://www.nature.com/news/2010/100602/full/465540a.html

preserve, and restore it for coming generations. They must reduce greenhouse gas emissions, control overfishing, ensure sustainable aquaculture, and stop sewage overflows and non-point pollution to protect the earth's waters. If they do so, "it shall be that everything that moves, wherever the rivers go, will live. There will be a very great multitude of fish, because these waters go there; for they will be healed, and everything will live wherever the river goes." Ezekiel 47:9. If not, "the land will mourn; and everyone who dwells there will waste away with the beasts of the field and the birds of the air; even the fish of the sea will be taken away." Hosea 4:3

Chapter 11: Metamorphosis of the Media

———

F *ocus on how to be social, not on how to do social.*

—-*Jay Baer, Convince & Convert*

The perpetrators of the attempted murder of the earth and its waters described in the last two chapters are climate change deniers and propagandists for polluting industries. Abetted by right-wing broadcast networks and social media, they dismiss the science warning us of the dangers of global warming as a hoax. The honest, fact-based journalism that energized my career in public service has metamorphosed into a vast conduit of misinformation and disinformation.

During my time in public office, honest and reputable print and broadcast media assisted me at critical points. They accurately reported the lies and misrepresentations of my political opponents. They exposed corruption in municipal, county, and state government. Reporters asked good questions and probed further for complete answers. They also opined about the good or the bad of issues I grappled with—public transportation, racism, pollution, family dissolution, prisoner reentry, climate change, and many others. There were no complaints about "fake news" or "witch hunts."

Beginning near the end of the 20th Century and continuing in the 21st, social media irreversibly changed the national and local political landscape. The machinations of Charles and David Koch, compelling right-wing rhetoric of Fox News, and rantings of syndicated talk show hosts like Glenn Beck and Rush Limbaugh fueled the politically fundamentalist Tea Party. Three components—elite organizations, conservative media, and local groups of everyday citizens—connected through social and mass media to create the Tea Party network that ended my political career in 2010.[126]

This right-wing media cabal is damaging the political life of the nation. Social media platforms are using algorithms to decide what videos and stories a user is most likely to enjoy based on past content watched or engaged with. Online readership is siphoning off subscription and advertising revenue that supported local newspapers. 2,900 newspapers have gone out of business, and the country has lost almost two-thirds of its newspaper journalists — 43,000 since 2005. As a result, residents in more than half of U.S. counties have no, or extremely limited, access to a reliable local news source — either print, digital or broadcast.[127]

Meanwhile, social media has burgeoned because of its ability to link countless users easily any time and everywhere. It spreads free information globally and makes it simple for people to interact with one another. But it has biases, sensationalizes information, is addictive, and consumes a lot of time. Content recommendation algorithms spread disinformation. They incentivize and reward extreme and sensationalist content that is increasingly empowering division, xenophobia, neo-Nazism, racism, misogyny, antisemitism, and authoritarianism. In sum, the metamorphosis, or more accurately, the regression, of the media represents an extraordinary change in the character of our national discourse for the worse. [128]

Section 230 of the 1996 Communications Decency Act (CDA) states that "no provider or user of an interactive computer service shall be treated as the publisher or speaker of any information provided by another information content provider." Under this shield, dangerous platforms such as Instagram, Facebook, Meta, X, Snapchat, TikTok, Tumblr, Telegram, and Tinder are helping radical individuals, foreign enemies, and fringe groups like Q-Anon to dominate national conversation. Without the restraint of traditional journalistic rules for vetting and reporting news, social media platforms and some broadcast networks have become fertile ground for "fake news" and propaganda. They have caused crazy ideas, lies, and conspiracy theories to spread more rapidly than facts. In 2016, they facilitated the election of Donald Trump, who made over 30,000 false statements during his four years as President of the United States; [129] and they continue to propagate his lies about climate change, voter fraud, and a host of other issues.

Thomas Jefferson emphasized the importance of newspapers as mediators of facts and gatekeeper of truth:

> The basis of our government being the opinion of the people, the very first object should be to keep that right; and were it left to me to decide whether we should have a government without newspapers, or newspapers without government, I should not hesitate to prefer the latter. [130]

The diminution of responsible print journalism is perverting participatory democracy. Former Senator Bill Bradley spells out the consequences:

> The losers here are the people who would like to know: What happened in the city council meeting? Or in the congressional committee room? How was the money for schools spent? How did that special-interest tax break make it into the tax code? Who agreed to the pensions that bankrupted our town? What did corporation X do for the ten thousand workers it just fired? How will the latest technological innovation affect jobs?... Without facts to challenge a government official or a CEO, the people's questions and accusations are parried by elementary public-relations tactics. [131]

According to the Rand Corporation, without some kind of government intervention, social media companies are unlikely to self-regulate effectively. The question is how can regulation by a federal agency, holding platforms liable for their content in civil court or requiring data transparency and reporting, bring about structural change without compromising the democratic tradition of free speech? Federal regulation would require a new law from Congress that would give authority over social media to an agency housed within the executive branch. Another option would be to revise Section 230 of the CDA to establish that courts can hold social media companies liable for harm caused by content on their platforms. This option would run headlong into the US Supreme Court ruling in *Reno v. ACLU,* [132] which held that internet companies are unlike traditional publishers. Because internet companies at the time of the ruling did not choose who was authoring posts or typing away in chat rooms, the court said they were not legally responsible for their content in the same way as *The New York Times* or *Washington Post,* which decide whether to publish each article. The counter argument is that it is the companies' algorithms that are substantially responsible[1] for what is, and is not, amplified[2] on their platforms.

The Rand report notes that "individuals can sue traditional media companies for damages because the company promulgated the defamatory content. Are social media platforms any less responsible for viral and promoted content?" Finally, the report says Congress could require greater transparency by passing laws such as the pending Platform Accountability and Transparency Act, which would require social media platforms to make data available to third-party researchers and evaluators. In theory, scrutiny by independent researchers might encourage social media companies to do a better job containing the spread of malicious information. [133]

Meanwhile, the situation may get worse! The development and rapid improvement of Artificial Intelligence (AI) threatens to gut the news business further and foster the rise of disinformation. Human norms, values, and reasonable assumptions do not constrain AI. [134] They will not deter our foreign enemies or domestic evildoers from fabricating the actions and speech of politicians and influential persons. Fake ads that appear genuine will proliferate in future elections if not somehow detected and curbed.

There are international attempts to regulate AI. In 2019, countries belonging to the Organization for Economic Co-operation and Development (OECD) adopted nonbinding principles[3] laying out values that should underpin AI development. They provide that AI systems should be transparent and explainable; should function in a robust, secure, and safe way; should have accountability mechanisms; and should respect the rule of law, human rights, democratic values, and diversity. The International Organization for Standardization (ISO) has developed standards for how companies should

---

1. https://www.science.org/toc/science/381/6656

2. https://www.nature.com/articles/d41586-023-02325-x

3. https://oecd.ai/en/ai-principles

implement risk management[4] and impact assessments[5] and manage the development[6] of AI. In 2021, the UN agency UNESCO and member countries adopted a voluntary AI ethics framework. Member countries pledge to introduce ethical impact assessments for AI, assess its environmental impact, ensure that it promotes gender equality and prohibit its use for mass surveillance. The problem with many of these efforts is that each country must ratify treaties individually and then implement them in national law, which could take years. Countries like China and Russia, which have used AI to surveil people, might opt out of stringent rules or moratoriums they dislike. [135]

The European Union is implementing an AI Act[7] that will regulate the most "high-risk" uses of AI systems. Recognizing the potential threat to citizens' rights and democracy posed by certain applications of AI, the Act prohibits:

◈ Biometric categorization systems that use sensitive characteristics (e.g., political, religious, philosophical beliefs, sexual orientation, race).

◈ Untargeted scraping of facial images from the internet or CCTV footage to create facial recognition databases.

◈ Emotion recognition in the workplace and educational institutions.

◈ Social scoring based on social behavior or personal characteristics.

◈ AI systems that manipulate the behavior of humans to circumvent their free will; and

◈ AI used to exploit the vulnerabilities of people due to their age, disability, social or economic situation.

4. https://www.iso.org/standard/77304.html

5. https://www.iso.org/standard/81230.html

6. https://www.iso.org/standard/81230.html

7. https://www.technologyreview.com/2022/05/13/1052223/guide-ai-act-europe/

The Act allows law enforcement to use biometric identification systems only in public spaces for certain crimes. It includes transparency requirements for all general-purpose AI models, like OpenAI's GPT-4, which powers ChatGPT. Companies violating the rules can be fined up to 7 percent of their global turnover. [136]

The US is trying to develop domestic AI regulations. President Joe Biden issued an Executive Order in 2023 that requires developers of the most powerful AI systems share their safety test results and other critical information with the U.S. government. It requires the National Institute of Standards and Technology to create standards to ensure AI tools are safe and secure before public release. The Commerce Department is to issue guidance to label and watermark AI-generated content to help differentiate between authentic interactions and those generated by software. The executive order also directs federal agencies and government departments to develop standards for AI. [137] We need more. Absent federal legislation, the US cannot present a model for how to move forward globally with AI governance. Instead, we must simply react to the approaches of other countries, such as the EU AI Act, regarding AI regulation. [138]

There was no television in my home until I was ten years old and a limited selection of TV programs into my teen years. When my siblings, friends, and I were home, we read books, magazines, and newspapers. When we were outside, we played baseball, football, and other sports and enjoyed the outdoors together. We maintained these habits into adulthood because we had become accustomed to that way of life. Not so with today's youth and young adults. Cell phones and social media have co-opted reading and are leading to a loss of literacy, dulling critical thinking skills, and vitiating civil engagement and civility. While social media may benefit some children and adolescents, mounting evidence shows that social media can harm their mental health and well-being. [139]

Multiple states and the federal government have passed or proposed legislation to protect children's safety online. These measures have different platform exemptions and requirements for age verification and parental consent that create a disjointed patchwork of regulation. Big tech companies, such as Amazon, Google, Meta, Yahoo, and TikTok are challenging individual state efforts. NetChoice, a lobbying organization that represents large tech firms, has filed lawsuits to overturn state laws.

Two bipartisan bills to protect children's internet use are pending in Congress. The Kids Online Safety Act (KOSA) would create new guidance for the Federal Trade Commission (FTC) and state Attorney Generals to penalize companies that expose children to harmful content on their platforms, including those that glamorize eating disorders, suicide, and substance abuse, among other such behaviors. An updated Children Online Privacy Protection Act (COPPA 2.0) would amend the existing COPPA, which protects the privacy of children under the age of thirteen by requesting parental consent for the collection or use of any personal information of the users. COPPA 2.0 would raise the age from 13 to 16 and establish bans on companies that advertise to kids.

Overall, industry and civil society organizations should welcome comprehensive federal legislation establishing a duty of care, baseline standards, and safeguards over a patchwork of state laws. A federal law could establish more consistent and certain definitions around age and verification methods, parental consent rules, privacy protections through limits on data collection, and enforcement by the FTC and state Attorney General offices. A federal foundation would allow states to add protections narrowly tailored to local contexts. [140]

While we wait for federal action, it is critical that we enhance the "actual" intelligence of the 95% of youth who use social media platforms. New Jersey Governor Phil Murphy has taken a crucial step to educate and protect the next generation that merits emulation. On January 3, 2023, he signed a law requiring media literacy for grades K to twelve. [141] Advocates say the measure will help students bombarded with information from social media and news outlets learn how to discern whether the sources are credible. The law requires the state Department of Education to implement literacy curriculum standards. These include research, using critical thinking skills, and learning the difference between facts and opinions and between primary and secondary sources. Governor Murphy said, "K-12 media literacy education will empower future leaders to accurately assess information — essential in preserving our democracy in a time of disinformation."

You must also take action to combat online disinformation to preserve the planet and our republic.[142]

Chapter 12: Preventing the Murder of American Democracy

The nation blessed above all nations is she in whom the civic genius of the people does the saving day by day… by speaking, writing, voting reasonably; by smiting corruption swiftly; by good temper between parties; by the people knowing true men when they see them, and preferring them as leaders to rabid partisans or empty quacks.

—*William James*

I thought I had put behind me the memory of the two murders with which my careers as a lawyer and public servant had a tangential beginning. I never expected that in the twilight of my years, I would witness not only the attempted murder of the planet on land and sea, but also the attempted murder of American democracy. The two crimes are interconnected. A stable United States government committed to sustaining and expanding environmental and energy programs and policies combatting global warming is required to restore the key life support functions mentioned at the beginning of Chapter 9. As the world's leading economic power, the US is the only country rich enough to fund the global efforts required to save the planet. Planetary salvation cannot be achieved, however, if America fails to get its domestic affairs in order and loses its Constitution and democratic institutions.

Between 1964 and 2016, the United States adopted far reaching laws and regulations to curtail air and water pollution, clean up toxic wastes, protect ecosystems, and reduce energy use. It also secured international agreements addressing global environmental problems. These policies and initiatives had widespread, bipartisan public support. Unfortunately, in the 21st Century, campaigns fueled by social media have tried to delegitimize the underlying evidence justifying environmental policies by labeling it as "junk science" or a "hoax." Presidential administrations and Congresses have vacillated between supporting expansion of environmental protection and weakening or even reversing them. The election of Donald Trump in 2016, along with conservative majorities in both houses of Congress, ushered in a hostile and wide-ranging attack on environmental policy and American democracy. [143]

On January 6, 2021, Trump aroused a mob of hundreds of his supporters to break into the US Capitol to prevent the peaceful transfer of power to President Joe Biden. The rioters chased senators and representatives into hiding and injured over 110 police officers. Five people died during the incident. Although charged with numerous felonies stemming from this insurrection, Trump continued to assert that he should be reinstated as President, arguing that "massive fraud" in the 2020 election justified nullification of all rules, regulations, and articles, including those in the Constitution. His Make America Great Again (MAGA) adherents remained silent as Trump offered authoritarianism to the American people as a substitute for Constitutional democracy.

To meet this challenge and to prevent the murder of American democracy, US citizens must be prepared to answer critical questions:

What are the basic principles of American Democracy?

On my first day in her class, my eleventh-grade Social Studies teacher Elisabeth Kelley at Red Bank High School asked us to describe the basic principles of democracy. Of course, we could not, so a large part of the curriculum for the year involved discussing, analyzing, and learning them. At the end of the year, Kelley told us that our final exam would include the question, "what are the basic principles of American Democracy?" I am proud to say that I aced the exam, and the principles have stuck with me ever since. Can you, your family, and your friends and acquaintances answer Elisabeth Kelley's question? If so, congratulations! If not, I suggest you turn to Exhibit A before reading any further.

The underlying ideas of American democracy can be found in the Declaration of Independence, the Preamble of the Constitution, Article I, Section 8 of the Constitution, and the 1st, 4th, 6th, 7th, 14th, 15th, 19th, and 26th Amendments. Influenced by ancient Greek philosophers and by English and French thinkers of the Age of Enlightenment[1], Thomas Jefferson placed this illustrious sentence in the Declaration of Independence: "We hold these truths to be self-evident, that all men are created equal." With the end of slavery in 1865, and the enfranchisement of women in 1920, Jefferson's words came to mean that all human beings are by nature equal as persons.

The Declaration states that all human beings "are endowed by their Creator with certain inalienable rights, that among these are life, liberty, and the pursuit of happiness." The Declaration states that to secure these rights, "governments are instituted among men, deriving their just powers from the consent of the governed." The founding fathers considered the pursuit of happiness to be the primary right guaranteed by the Declaration. John Adams believed that "the happiness of society is the end of government." [144] Jefferson agreed, declaring that "the care of human life and happiness, and not their destruction, is the first and only legitimate object of good government." [145] These Presidents derived their concept of happiness from Aristotle, who believed that "happiness is the meaning and purpose of life, the whole aim and end of human existence." It encompasses a whole life well-lived and enriched by the cumulative possession of all the goods — health, sufficient wealth, knowledge, friendship, and virtue — that a moral and ethical human being ought to desire. [146]

Conservative 20th Century philosopher and educator Mortimer Adler added that by virtue of common humanity, all human beings "have an equal right to life, liberty, and whatever else anyone naturally needs for success in the pursuit of happiness. Should individuals be unable to secure for themselves whatever is thus needed, then a just government is called upon to secure for them their right to these goods" [147] Toward that end, the Preamble of the Constitution declares that "We, the people of the United States, in order to form a more perfect union, establish justice, insure domestic tranquility, provide for the common defense, promote the general welfare, and secure the blessings of liberty to ourselves and our posterity, do ordain and establish this Constitution for the United States of America." The first clause of Section 8 of the Constitution gives Congress the power to lay and collect taxes and acquire

1. https://en.wikipedia.org/wiki/Age_of_Enlightenment

other revenues. It can use these to pay the nation's debts and to provide for the "common defense and general welfare of the United States." Later in this chapter, I discuss how presidents and congresses have implemented this power.

Is the United States a "Christian" Nation?

According to the Pew Research Center, "most Americans think the founders of America intended for the US to be a 'Christian nation,' more than four-in-ten think the United States should be a Christian nation, and a third say the country is a Christian nation today. However, Americans' views of what it means to be a Christian nation are wide-ranging and often ambiguous. To some, being a Christian nation implies Christian-based laws and governance. For others it means the subtle guidance of Christian beliefs and values in everyday life, or even simply a population with faith in something bigger." Just under half of Americans say the Bible should have some influence on US laws.[148]

Congressman Mike Johnson, who was elected as Speaker of the House of Representatives in 2023, promotes the notion that the United States is a "Christian nation" and has called for "biblically sanctioned government." A "Christian" is a person who has repented of his or her sins and put faith and trust in the person and work of Jesus Christ, including His death on the cross as payment for them. (1 John 1.9). His resurrection on the third day is for Christians a signal that Jesus is the powerful Son of God who has conquered death and reigns as Lord of all. (Romans 1:4; 1 Corinthians 8.6). The mark of a true Christian is love for others (1 John 2:10) in imitation of Christ (1 Corinthians 11.1).

The founding fathers were Deists (believers in God as creator of, but having no control over, the universe) rather than Christians, and they provided in the First Amendment to the Constitution that "Congress shall make no law respecting an establishment of religion or prohibiting the free exercise thereof." They were nevertheless aware of the importance of Christian values. In the Virginia Bill of Rights from which Jefferson drew inspiration, Patrick Henry said "it is the mutual duty of all to practice Christian forbearance, love, and charity towards each other."[149]

Thomas Jefferson regarded himself as "a real Christian – that is to say, a disciple of the doctrines of Jesus Christ." [150] His version of the Bible, which only contained the words of Jesus, included this passage:

> Then shall the King say to those on his right hand, "Come, you blessed of My Father, inherit the kingdom prepared for you from the foundation of the world: for I was hungry and you gave Me food; I was thirsty and you gave Me drink; I was a stranger and you took Me in; I was naked and you clothed Me; I was sick and you visited Me; I was in prison and you came to Me. Then the righteous will answer Him, saying, Lord, when did we see You hungry and feed You, or thirsty and give You drink? When did we see You a stranger and take You in, or naked and clothe you? Or when did we see You sick, or in prison, and come to You. And the King will answer and say to them, assuredly, I say to you, inasmuch as you did it unto one of the least of these My brethren, you did it to Me. (Matthew 25:34-40)

Before becoming President, Abraham Lincoln recognized the compatibility of the Declaration of Independence with Christianity in an 1858 speech in Lewiston, Illinois:

> This was their majestic interpretation of the economy of the Universe. This was their lofty, wise, and noble understanding of the justice of the Creator to His creatures. Yes, gentlemen, to all His creatures, to the whole great family of man. In their enlightened belief, nothing stamped with the Divine image and likeness was sent into the world to be trodden on, and degraded, and imbruted by its fellows.... Wise statesmen as they were, they knew the tendency of prosperity to breed tyrants, and so they established these great self-evident truths, that when in the distant future some man, some faction, some interest, should set up the doctrine that none but rich men, or none but white men, were entitled to life, liberty, and pursuit of happiness, their posterity might look up again to the Declaration of Independence and take courage to renew the battle which their fathers began – so that truth, justice, mercy, and all the

humane and Christian virtues might not be extinguished from the land; so that no man would hereafter dare to limit and circumscribe the great principles on which the temple of liberty was being built.

For more than a century, past presidents and congresses have followed Christian precepts and promoted the "general welfare" of the nation by protecting the life and health of its citizens and acting charitably toward the less fortunate. President Theodore Roosevelt recognized that "the object of the government is the welfare of the people" and that "the material progress and prosperity of a nation are desirable chiefly so far as they lead to the moral and material welfare of all good citizens." [151] His domestic program had three basic ideas known as the "three C's": conservation of natural resources, control of corporations, and consumer protection. He fought for a "Square Deal" for all Americans, meaning an equal chance for all to succeed. He regulated big business trusts, established the Department of Commerce and Labor, and enacted the Pure Food and Drug and Meat Inspection Acts to protect the public against impure foods. A dedicated conservationist, Roosevelt set aside two hundred million acres for national forests, reserves, and wildlife refuges and established five national parks, fifty-one federal sanctuaries for birds, four national game reserves, and eighteen national monuments, including the Grand Canyon.

President Franklin D. Roosevelt declared in his 1944 message to Congress that "true individual freedom cannot exist without economic security and independence ... People who are hungry and out of a job are the stuff of which dictatorships are made ..."[152] He urged Congress to implement various economic rights — to a useful and remunerative job, adequate food and shelter, a decent home, adequate medical care, a good education, and protection from the economic fears of old age, sickness, accident, and unemployment. Under his leadership, Congress enacted the Social Security Act of 1935, providing unemployment, disability, and old-age assistance and the National Labor Relations Act guaranteeing the basic rights of private sector employees to form unions. Other major legislation included the Housing Act of 1937 which provided subsidies to local public housing agencies to improve living conditions for low-income families and the Fair Labor Standards Act of 1938 which introduced the forty-hour work week, established a national minimum wage, guaranteed 1.5 times the hourly rate for overtime in certain jobs, and prohibited the employment of minors in oppressive child labor.

In his address to the National Association for the Advancement of Colored People (NAACP) in 1947 President Harry Truman said, "there is no justifiable reason for discrimination because of ancestry, or religion, or race, or color."[153] He then pushed forward the cause of American civil rights by desegregating the military, banning discrimination in the civil service, and commissioning a federal report on civil rights.

President Lyndon Johnson said in 1964 that "The challenge of the next half century is whether we have the wisdom to use [our] wealth to enrich and elevate our national life—and to advance the quality of American civilization."[154] Toward that end, his Administration passed the Civil Rights Act of 1964 outlawing discrimination based on race, color, religion, or national origin, and the Voting Rights Act of 1965. As part of his War on Poverty, he signed into law the Economic Opportunity Act, which created the Office of Economic Opportunity to coordinate federal antipoverty initiatives and empower the poor to transform their own communities. The Food Stamp Act addressed hunger and the Housing and Urban Development Act expanded funding for federal housing programs. Johnson amended the Social Security Act to create Medicare and Medicaid. Medicare gives health insurance to people over sixty-five and Medicaid helps low-income groups get medical care.

Johnson believed that education was a cure for ignorance and poverty. He therefore provided funding under the Elementary and Secondary Education Act to give each child an equal opportunity to achieve an exceptional education. The Higher Education Act of 1965 increased federal grants to universities, created scholarships, gave low-interest loans to students, and established a National Teachers Corps. Johnson also began the Head Start program that provides poor children with early education and nutrition.

President Richard Nixon said that "the Congress, the Administration, and the public all share a profound commitment to the rescue of our natural environment, and the preservation of the Earth as a place both habitable by and hospitable to man." [155] Although impeached like Trump, albeit only once, he deserves credit for creating the Environmental Protection Agency and enacting the Endangered Species Act, the National Environmental Policy Act, the Clean Air Act of 1970, and the Marine Mammal Protection Act of 1972. He also proposed the Safe Drinking Water Act, which his successor, President Gerald Ford, signed into law.

President Barack Obama said that "if the people cannot trust their government to do the job for which it exists - to protect them and to promote their common welfare - all else is lost." [156] His signature achievement was the Affordable Care Act extending health coverage to approximately thirty-two million Americans and cutting health care costs.

These outstanding achievements of past presidents are consistent with the purposes and objectives of the Declaration of Independence, the Constitution, and Christianity. They have safeguarded our "inalienable rights" to life, liberty, and the pursuit of happiness. They have helped us form a more perfect union, establish justice, promote general welfare, and secure the blessings of liberty to current and future generations.

Is the government the Republican Party, Donald Trump, and his MAGA supporters want to establish consistent with the core values and ideals of the Declaration of Independence, the Constitution, and Christianity?

If restored to power, we can expect the Republican Party and its Trump led MAGA supporters, to govern the same way the Administration of former President Donald Trump did when in power. Trump's great achievements, in the eyes of many evangelicals, include moving the U.S. Embassy in Israel from Tel Aviv to Jerusalem, and – more profoundly – appointing three Supreme Justices who have helped repeal the nationwide right to abortion[2]. Trump's concern for the unborn was not coupled, however, with compassion for the born. From 2017 to 2020, his Administration pursued restrictions on the government's role in regulating health care, environmental protection, gun control, employment, and the social safety net. It weakened worker rights and workplace safety, curtailed the Affordable Care Act, eviscerated public health

2. https://apnews.com/article/abortion-dobbs-anniversary-state-laws-51c2a83899f133556e715342abfcface

safeguards, and rolled back rules governing clean air, water, and toxic chemicals. The Trump administration's chaotic and mismanaged response to the coronavirus crisis cost more than 200,000 Americans their lives. Trump also dismantled major climate policies and wildlife protections, cut federal affordable housing programs, and reduced federal oversight of, and support for, public education and protection of student rights. Meanwhile, he added three trillion dollars to the national debt by reducing taxes on the rich and large corporations.

This record is contrary to the teachings of Jesus Christ about helping the poor, sick and needy. It is also at variance with Biblical Christianity: "But whoever has this world's goods, and sees his brother in need, and shuts up his heart from him, how does the love of God abide in him?" 1 John 3:17. The MAGA approach to governing reflects instead a libertarian, "Tea Party" view that emphasizes individual liberty in personal and economic affairs without interference from government. It asserts that government should not exercise power over the marketplace and the economic decisions and interests of individuals and corporations, even if the result is that some citizens are impoverished.

President Joe Biden and the Democratic Party took the opposite approach. They reversed many of the actions of the Trump Administration, and they resisted MAGA efforts to shred the social safety net comprising Social Security, Obamacare, Medicaid, Medicare, the Supplemental Nutrition Assistance Program (SNAP), and other welfare programs. President Biden's operating principle was, "There are some days when we need a hand. There are other days when we're called on to lend one. That is how we must be with one another. And, if we are this way, our country will be stronger, more prosperous, more ready for the future."[157] This statement reflects the principle, implicit in the founding documents and the thinking of our founding fathers, that there should be a balance between liberty and equality. Thomas Jefferson expressed it this way: "rightful liberty is unobstructed action according to our will within limits drawn around us by the equal rights of others."[158]

In his book *Six Great Ideas,* Mortimer Adler wrote that the nation's founders recognized that "neither liberty nor equality...is an unlimited good, and that both can be maximized harmoniously only when regulated by justice." Our elected representatives should therefore make sure that we have as much liberty as justice allows and as much equality of conditions as justice requires. The economic inequality that justice allows "consists in some having more wealth than anyone needs ... but since the amount of wealth available for distribution is limited, no one should be in a position to earn by his productive contribution — to earn, not to steal or seize — so much wealth that not enough remains for distribution, in one way or another, to put all individuals on the baseline of economic sufficiency." Justice requires that no individual or family be "seriously deprived, by destitution or dire poverty, of that minimal supply of economic goods that everyone needs.... To this much everyone has a natural right."[159]

This formulation aligns with the principles of the New Testament and the Torah, which describe the balance between liberty and equality toward which American democracy must strive:

> Of course, I don't mean your giving should make life easy for others and hard for yourselves. I only mean that there should be some equality. Right now, you have plenty and can help those who are in need. Later, they will have plenty and can share with you when you need it. In this way, things will be equal. (2 Corinthians 8:13-15, New Living Translation). As it is written, the one who gathered much did not have too much, and the one who gathered little did not have too little. Exodus 16:18, Revised Standard Version.

What should we do to prevent the murder of the American democratic republic?

The battle to save the American democratic republic must be fought on three fronts. First, we must elect candidates for national, state, and local office who understand and support the Constitution. We should support candidates who promise to address the vast inequality that prevails today in the United States, where the wealthiest 1 percent of families hold about 40 percent of all wealth, and the bottom 90 percent of families hold less than one-quarter.[160] They must be willing to help the millions of American families and children who live below the poverty line, are food insecure, and lack health insurance; and the more than half a million who are homeless. They must be willing to fight bigotry, antisemitism, autocracy, and racism; and they must support local, national, and international efforts to prevent the murder of the planet.

Second, we must stop the political misuse of wealth and power and enact reforms that fully implement government "by consent of the governed" as envisioned in the Declaration of Independence. The MAGA dominated Republican Party is supported by the rich Americans and hugely profitable corporations that benefit from low effective rates of taxation and tax loopholes. They employ every means, including populating the Supreme Court and Federal Judiciary with their hand-picked collaborators, to reduce the size of government and overturn laws and regulations they disfavor. They promote their agenda by feeding the public a steady dose of lies and disinformation through the right-wing broadcast and social media outlets they control. Their power comes from the hundreds of millions of dollars they pour into the national and state campaigns of candidates on whose support they can rely.

We must enact reforms that will put an end to big money's stranglehold on democracy. These include public financing of campaigns, abolishing the electoral college, electing the President by popular vote, and ending gerrymandering, We should also protect the integrity of the electoral system by outlawing unreasonable and unnecessary impediments to the right to vote, such as unreasonable limitations on voting by mail, overly burdensome identification requirements, and unduly restrictive times and places for the exercise of the franchise. [161] In the words of President Abraham Lincoln, these steps are required so "that government of the people, by the people, for the people shall not perish from the earth." [162]

Third, we must reverse the degeneration of the politics of the nation by addressing widespread public ignorance of the historical and philosophical origins and functions of American democracy. Americans have limited civics knowledge, one in four being unable to name the three branches of government. Confidence in our political leadership is extremely low. As of March 2019, only seventeen percent trusted the government in Washington to do the right thing. [163] This troubling statistic calls to mind Thomas Jefferson's warning that "if a nation expects to be ignorant and free, in a state of civilization, it expects what never was and never will be." [164]

The American public school system must do a better job teaching history and civics. Just 13 percent of the nation's eighth graders were proficient in U.S. history in 2022, and only 22 percent were proficient in civics, sounding an alarm about how well students understand their country and its government. [165] Most states have dedicated insufficient class time to understanding the basic functions of government at the expense of other courses, and only a few states currently provide sufficient and comprehensive civic education. [166]

Improvement of civics education in the United States is imperative because, as John Adams said,

> Liberty cannot be preserved without a general knowledge among the people, who have a right, from the frame of their nature to knowledge, as their great Creator who does nothing in vain, has given them understandings, and a desire to know—but besides this they have a right, an indisputable, unalienable, indefeasible divine right to that most dreaded, and envied kind of knowledge, I mean of the characters and conduct of their rulers. Rulers are no more than attorneys, agents, and trustees for the people; and if the cause, the interest and trust is insidiously betray'd, or wantonly trifled away, the people have a right to revoke the authority, that they themselves have deputed, and to constitute abler and better agents, attorneys and trustees. And the preservation of the means of knowledge, among the lowest ranks, is of more importance to the public than all the property of all the rich men in the country. [167]

U.S. government, civics, or service-learning education must teach students "to systemically address issues in their communities; civics exams must address critical thinking, in addition to comprehension of materials; and civics and government courses should prepare every student with the tools to become engaged and effective citizens." Colorado has designed detailed curricula that are taught throughout yearlong courses. Colorado teachers are expected to cover the origins of democracy, the structure of American government, methods of public participation, a comparison to foreign governments, and the responsibilities of citizenship. The Colorado Department of Education also provides content, guiding questions, key skills, and vocabulary as guidance for teachers. In addition, Colorado teachers help civics come alive in the classroom through the Judicially Speaking program, which was started by three local judges to teach students how judges think through civics as they make decisions. [168] This approach should be followed in other states.

The attack on the US Capitol on January 6, 2021, was a shocking reminder that our republic is very fragile. Those who tried to impede the Congressional certification of the 2020 election exhibited a dangerous lack of knowledge of and concern for the basic principles of American democracy, and they will keep trying to undermine and abrogate them. Therefore, if you share my love of American democracy and want to protect, preserve, and strengthen it, you must take part in the process of government as I have done throughout my career. Pray and meditate about the best way you can act to bring about change. Focus on the issues or causes about which you have passionate feelings. Many references in this book can open the door to further inquiry. Thoroughly study what interests you. Once you have decided on a course of action, connect with other people, and join and contribute to people and organizations that are working on the same subjects. Share your views in hearings, attend meetings, and take part in peaceful protests. Do not quit until you win.

If we care and act, we can achieve a positive metamorphosis of American democracy and preserve a sustainable planet for our children, grandchildren, and future generations. I pray that you will take the examples and messages of this book to heart and work toward those ends with the assurance that "God is able to make all grace abound toward you, that you, always having all sufficiency in all things, may have an abundance for every good work." 2 Corinthians 9:8

Appendix A

———

Here is Elisabeth Kelley's list of the basic principles of democracy:

1. All people are created equal.

2. All persons are endowed with natural rights, including life, liberty, the pursuit of happiness, and the ownership of property.

3. The people are guaranteed freedom of religion, speech, assembly, the press, and the right to petition the government for redress of grievances.

4. No person can be deprived of life, liberty, or property without due process of law, including trial by jury.

5. Government is by consent of the governed by democratically elected representatives (the highest vote getter being sworn into office).

6. The people may change their government by amending the constitution from which it derives its powers.

Endnotes

---

[1]

Unless otherwise noted, all biblical quotations in this book are from the New King James Version (NKJV)

[2] Detwiler, Donald S. *Germany: A Short History*. Southern Illinois University Press, 1999, p. 43.

[3] Arloc Sherman, Danilo Trisi, Chad Stone, Shelby Gonzales, and Sharon Parrott, *Immigrants Contribute Greatly to U.S. Economy, Despite Administration's "Public Charge" Rule Rationale,* Center on Budget and Policy Priorities, August 15, 2019, https://www.cbpp.org/research/immigrants-contribute-greatly-to-us-economy-despite-administrations-public-charge-rule

[4] The testimony of the key witnesses in the Coppolino trial is detailed by Paul Holmes in *The Trials of Dr. Coppolino,* Signet Books published by The New American Library, Inc., 1968, pp. 122-197

[5] The testimony of the scientific and medical experts is detailed by Paul Holmes in *The Trials of Dr. Coppolino,* supra, pp.223-257.

[6] Coppolino v. State, 223 So.2d 68 (Fla App, 1969), app dis 234 So.2d 120 (Fla, 1969, cert denied 399 U.S.927 (1970)

[7] Daubert v. Merrell Dow Pharmaceuticals, Inc., 509 U.S. 579, 590 (1993)

[8] In the Matter of Commuter Operating Agency's Determination of Financial Results to Carriers for the Calendar Year 1977, 164 NJ Super 11 (1978)

[9] James Boswell, *Life of Samuel Johnson* (1791) 19 September 1777

[10] New Jersey Statutes Annotated, 27:1B-1, et seq.

[11] John D'Amico, Jr, *Subsidizing Mass Transit,* The New York Times, New Jersey Opinion, December 19, 1982, p.38

[12] International Energy Agency, *Energy Efficiency 2020*, IEA, Paris https://www.iea.org/reports/energy-efficiency-2020

[13] Opinion: *"More Republicans seem to have lied about their resumes. Who's surprised?"* Jennifer Rubin, The Washington Post, February 20, 2023

[14] https://cleanoceanaction.org

[15] American Farmland Trust, *"Farmlands Under Threat,"* 2022, https://farmlandinfo.org/wp-content/uploads/sites/2/2022/08/AFT_FUT_Abundant-Future-7_29_22-WEB.pdf

[16] Woody Allen, *My Speech to the Graduates,* The New York Times, August 10, 1979.

[17] The US Department of Housing and Urban Development, The 2023 Annual Homelessness Assessment Report (AHAR to Congress), https://www.huduser.gov/portal/sites/default/files/pdf/2023-AHAR-Part-1.pdf

[18] Centers for Disease Control and Prevention, *"Homelessness as a Public Health Law Issue: Selected Resources,"* March 2, 2007, https://www.cdc.gov/phlp/publications/topic/resources/resources-homelessness.html

[19] Caitlin LaCroix and Kaitlyn Ranney, Community Solutions Policy Brief, *Land Use Regulations Local Zoning Ordinances, and Homelessness,* June 12, 2023, Home - Community Solutions[1], https://community.solutions/research-posts/policy-brief-land-use-regulations-local-zoning-ordinances-and-homelessness/

---

1. https://community.solutions/

[20] New Jersey Assembly Bill A4755, P.L.2023, c.62.

[21] Gale, *"Racism and White Supremacy in America,"* https://www.gale.com/ primary-sources/political-extremism-and-radicalism/collections/racism-and-white-supremacy

[22] United Nations Convention on Biological Diversity, Montreal Canada, December 18, 2022, https://www.unep.org/un-biodiversity-conference-cop-15

[23] US Department of the Interior, *America the Beautiful,* https://www.doi.gov/priorities/america-the-beautiful

[24] *C* & A Carbone, Inc. v. Town of Clarkstown, New York, 511 U.S. 383, 386 (1994)

[25] Alex Truelove, *America Has a Trash Problem,* PIRG, www.pirg.org

[26] Tiffany Duong, *"The Recycling Industry in America Is Broken"* EcoWatch, Apr 20, 2021, https://www.ecowatch.com/us-recycling-industry-2652630035.html

[27] Jordan B. Howell, *Garbage in the Garden State,* Rutgers University Press, 2023

[28] New Jersey Statutes Annotated (N.J.S.A.) 2C:39-5.

[29] N.J.S.A.2C:43-6.

[30] Gius, Mark (2015). *"The impact of state and federal assault weapons bans on public mass shootings".* Applied Economics Letters[2]. 22 (4): 281–284, https://www.researchgate.net/publication/271939348_The_impact_of_state_and_federal_assault_weapons_bans_on_public_m DiMaggio, C; Avraham, J; Berry, C; Bukur, M; Feldman, J; Klein, M; Shah, N; Tandon, M; Frangos, S (January 2019). *"Changes in US mass shooting deaths*

2. https://en.wikipedia.org/wiki/Applied_Economics_Letters

associated with the 1994–2004 federal assault weapons ban: Analysis of open-source data". The Journal of Trauma and Acute Care Surgery, 86, https://pubmed.ncbi.nlm.nih.gov/30188421/

[31] The Washington Post, Opinion: *"No one needs an AR-15 — or any gun tailor-made for mass shootings,"* March 28, 2023, https://www.washingtonpost.com/opinions/2023/03/28/ar-15-assault-rifles-magazines-ban/

[32] N.J.S.A. 58:10A-10.1 et al

[33] Oxford Languages, Oxford University Press, 2024

[34] Standard and Poors Global, *Climate Litigation: Assessing Potential Impacts Remains Complex,* May 7, 2024, www.spglobal.com[3]

[35] Brian D'Onofrio[4] and Robert Emery[5] *Parental divorce or separation and children's mental health,* World Psychiatry, February 18, 2019, https://www.ncbi.nlm.nih.gov/pmc/articles/PMC6313686/

[36] The American Academy of Child and Adolescent Psychiatry, *Children and Divorce,* January 2017, https://www.aacap.org/AACAP/Families_and_Youth/Facts_for_Families/FFF-Guide/Children-and-Divorce-001.aspx

[37] Catherine K. Buckley, PhD, *Co-Parenting after Divorce: Opportunities and Challenges,* The Family Institute at Northwestern University, 2013

[38] www.bsfinternational.org

[39] New Jersey Law Journal, family Law, November 13, 1995

---

3. http://www.spglobal.com

4. https://pubmed.ncbi.nlm.nih.gov/?term=D%27Onofrio%20B%5BAuthor%5D

5. https://pubmed.ncbi.nlm.nih.gov/?term=Emery%20R%5BAuthor%5D

[40] *Reality Checks for Alimony and Child Support*, New Jersey Law Journal, Family Law, September 18, 2000

[41] See New Jersey form of "Consent Order for Expedited Jury Trial" and jury instructions at www.judiciary.state.nj.us[6], by typing "Expedited Jury Trial" into the search box.

[42] Supreme Court of New Jersey, *"Code of Judicial Conduct,"* September 1, 2016

[43] N.J.S.A. 30:4-123.53(a)

[44] James Ahearn, *"Three good moves in Trenton,"* NorhJersey.com, October 5, 2003

[45] New Jersey reentry Roundtable Final Report, *Coming Home for Good: Meeting the Challenge of Prisoner Reentry Prisoner Reentry in New Jersey*, December 2023, New Jersey Institute for Social Justice, p.4

[46] Latessa, E., Cullen, F., and Gendreau, P, *Beyond Correctional Quackery—Professionalism*, Federal Probation, September 2002

[47] Yglesias, M. *The Research Wars.* The American Prospect, December 2003, 5-7, https://prospect.org/features/research-wars/

[48] National Institute on Drug Abuse, *Principles of Drug Addiction Treatment: A Research-Based Guide (Third Edition)*, January 2018, p.11

[49] Substance Abuse and Mental Health Services Administration. (2022). *Key substance use and mental health indicators in the United States: Results from the 2021 National Survey on Drug Use and Health* (HHS Publication No. PEP22-07-01-005, NSDUH Series H-57), pp 53-55, Center for Behavioral Health Statistics and Quality, Substance Abuse and Mental Health Services

Administration.   https://www.samhsa.gov/data/report/2021-nsduh-annual-national-report

[50] Emily Widra and Alexi Jones, *Mortality, health, and poverty: the unmet needs of people on probation and parole,* Prison Policy Initiative, April 3, 2023. https://www.prisonpolicy.org/blog/2023/04/03/nsduh_probaion_parole_

[51] Marushah, Laura; Bronson, Jennifer; and Alper Mariel, *Medical Problems Reported by Prisoners* (Survey of Prison Inmates, 2016); Bureau of Justice Statistics; June 2021,

[52] *"Improving Upon Corrections in New Jersey to Reduce Recidivism and Promote a Successful Reintegration,"* NJ Reentry Corporation, February 2017, p.6,   https://www.njreentry.org/application/files/7316/4089/3981/ Annual_Report_2017_Improving_Upon_Corrections.pdf

[53] http://www.voadv.org/promise

[54] *"This Camden halfway house is reducing recidivism across the river",* Billy Penn Reentry Project, May 11, 2017, https://billypenn.com/2017/05/11/ this-camden-halfway-house-is-reducing-recidivism-across-the-river/

[55] The healing effects of social connection and community are discussed in the U.S. Surgeon General's Advisory, *Our Epidemic of Loneliness and Isolation,* 2023

[56] American Psychological Association, *"What is Cognitive Behavioral Therapy?"* PTSD Clinical Practice Guideline, July 2017, https://www.apa.org/ ptsd-guideline/patients-and-families/cognitive-behavioral.pdf

[57] Joseph Bernsgtein, *"Back to the Couch with Freud,"* New New York Times, March   26,   2023,   https://www.nytimes.com/2023/03/22/style/ freud-psychoanalysis.html

[58] Hirchi, Travis, *Causes of Delinquency,* Berkeley: University University of California Press, 1969; Gottfredson, Michael R. and Hirchi, Travis, *A General Theory of Crime,* Stanford University Press, 1990

[59] Re-Entry Policy Council Report. 2005. *Charting the SafeAnd Successful Return of Prisoners to the Community, Re*-Entry Policy Council, U.S. Department of Justice, U.S. Department of Labor & U.S. Department of Health & Human Services, p. 204,

[60] Dana E. Sulliven, *Call it Faith Based Parole,* Jersey Dana E. Sulliven, *Call it Faith Based Parole,* New Jersey Lawyer, Volume 14, Number 35, August 29, 2005

[61] *Improving Upon Corrections...,"* NJ Reentry Corporation, February 2017, supra, p.9.

[62] New Jersey State Parole Board Annual Report for Fiscal Year 2020, p. 18

[63] N.J.S.A. 30:4-123.55b, et seq., "Earn Your Way Out Act," effective February 1, 2021

[64]Calculations based on DOC Fiscal Year 2018 Budget of $984,935,000 divided by 19,453 inmates and SPB Fiscal Year 2018 Budget of $97,152,000 divided by 15,000 parolees. "State of Recidivism," supra, pp. 25-26; "Max Out," supra, p. 7

[65] www.njreentry.org[7]

[66] Nancy M. Campbell, *"Comprehensive Framework for Paroling Authorities in an Era of Evidence-Based Practices,"* National Institute of Corrections, 2008, https://www.apaintl.org/_documents/surpub/framework.pdf

[67] Coleen O'Dea, *"New Jersey's Recidivism Rate Plummets 19 Percent over Past Six Years,"* N.J. Spotlight, November 15,2018,

---

7. http://www.njreentry.org

https://www.njspotlightnews.org/2018/11/18-11-14-new-jerseys-recidivism-rate-plummets-19-percent-over-past-six-years/

[68] National Institute on Drug Abuse, *Drug Overdose Death Rates,* 1999-2021, https://nida.nih.gov/research-topics/trends-statistics/overdose-death-rates

[69] Fact Sheet, Office of National Drug Control Policy, *Cost Benefits of Investing Early In Substance Abuse Treatment,* May 2012, https://obamawhitehouse.archives.gov/sites/default/files/ondcp/Fact_Sheets/investing_in_treatment_5-23-12.pdf

[70] The New York Times Opinion, *"America Has Lost the War on Drugs. What Now?"* February 26,2023, https://www.nytimes.com/2023/02/22/opinion/harm-reduction-public-health.html

[71] Call the New Jersey Department of Human Services at 1-844-ReachNJ[8], or contact https://www.preventioniskey.org/ in the northern region or https://preventionlinks.org/ in the central or southern regions of New Jersey

[72] Andrew Newberg, M.D. & Eugene D'Aquili, M.D. Ph. D, *Why God Won't Go Away: Brain Science and the Biology of Belief,* Ballantine Books, April 2001, p. 130; Bryan J. Grim and Melissa E. Grimm, *"Belief, Behavior, and Belonging: How Faith is Indispensable in Preventing and Recovering from Substance Abuse,"* Journal of Religion and Health, July 19, 2019,.

[73] https://www.tmewcf.org

[74] Re-Entry Policy Council Report, 2005, <u>supra,</u> p. 204

[75] Brian J. Grim and Melissa Grim, *Belief, Behavior, and Belonging,* <u>supra.</u>

[76] K Richardson, *Earth beyond six of nine planetary boundaries,* Science Advances, Volume 9, Issue 7, September 2023

[77] Leadership in Energy and Environmental Design, *LEED rating system,* https://www.usgbc.org/leed

[78] Climate Change News, *"The world's most polluting industries,"* May 11, 2023, https://climatetrade.com/the-worlds-most-polluting-industries/

[79] IPCC, 2007: *Climate Change 2007: Synthesis Report. Contribution of Working Groups I, II and III to the Fourth Assessment Report of the Intergovernmental Panel on Climate Change* [Core Writing Team, Pachauri, R.K and Reisinger, A. (eds.)]. IPCC, Geneva, Switzerland,

[80] New Jersey Department of Transportation *Complete Streets Policy,* December 3, 2009, https://www.state.nj.us/transportation/eng/completestreets/pdf/completestreetspolicy.pdf

[81] California Air Resources Board, https://ww2.arb.ca.gov/about

[82] Environmental Defense Fund, *A pioneering solution gets stronger,* Solutions, Vol 54, No 4, Fall 2023, https://www.edf.org/sites/default/files/2023-09/SOLUTIONS-Fall%202023.pdf

[83] Vijai Bhola, Attila Hertelendy, Alexander Hart, Syafwan Bin Adnan, Gregory Ciottone, *Escalating costs of billion-dollar disasters in the US: Climate change necessitates disaster risk reduction,* The Journal of Climate Change and Health[9], Volume 10[10], March–April 2023, https://www.sciencedirect.com/science/article/pii/S2667278222000906

[84] World Meteorological Organization, *State of the Global Climate 2022,* WMO-No. 1316, https://library.wmo.int/idurl/4/66214

[85] United States Environmental Protection Agency, *Climate Change Impacts on Coasts,* https://www.epa.gov/climateimpacts/climate-change-impacts-coasts

---

9. https://www.sciencedirect.com/journal/the-journal-of-climate-change-and-health

10. https://www.sciencedirect.com/journal/the-journal-of-climate-change-and-health/vol/10/suppl/C

[86] United Nations Conference of the Parties to the Paris

Agreement, *First global stocktake*, December 13, 2023

[87] Kevin Krajick, *A New 66 Million-Year History of Carbon Dioxide Offers Little Comfort for Today*, Columbia Climate School Lamont-Doherty earth Observatory, December 7, 2023

[88] AR6 Synthesis Report, *Climate Change 2023*, https://www.ipcc.ch/report/ar6/syr/longer-report

[89] Sara J. Scherr and Sajal Sthapit, *Farming and Land Use to Cool the Planet*, State of the World, The Worldwatch Institute, 2009, Chapter 3, https://www.preventionweb.net/files/7841_SOW09chap31.pdf

[90] Krystal Vasquez, *Fiddling With the Global*

Thermostat, Sierra, Vol.108, No.3, Fall 2023, p.64

[91] Sam Howe Verhovek, *Clearing the Air*, National Geographic, November 2023, p. 64

[92] International Energy Agency, *Electricity Grids and Secure Energy Transitions*, October 2023, https://www.iea.org/reports/electricity-grids-and-secure-energy-transitions

[93] 597 U.S. 697 (2022), 20-1530

[94] A Special Report, *The Energy Transition*, The New York Times, August 19, 2023, https://www.nytimes.com/spotlight/energy-transition

[95] New Jersey Department of Education, Student Learning Standards, 2020, https://www.nj.gov/education/cccs/2020/

[96] No. CDV-2020-307 (Mont. 1st Dist. Ct.) (14 Aug. 2023)

[97] Moore v. Harper, 600 U.S. 1 (2023)

[98] Richard Connor and Michela Miletto, *The United Nations World Water Development Report 2023: partnerships and cooperation for water,* UNESCO World Water Assessment Programme, https://www.unesco.org/reports/wwdr/2023/en

[99] World Economic Forum, *This is Why We Cannot Dismiss Water Scarcity in the US,* February 10,2023, https:www.weforum.org/agenda/2023/02/water-scarcity-united-states-un-water-conference/

[100] Mira Rojanasakul[11], Christopher Flavelle[12], Blacki Migliozzi[13] and Eli Murray[14], *America Is UsingUp Its Groundwater Like There's No Tomorrow,* New York Times, September 2, 2023, p. 14, https://www.nytimes.com/interactive/2023/08/28/climate/groundwater-drying-climate-change.html

[101] Chunyang He[15], Zhifeng Liu[16], Jianguo Wu[17], Xinhao Pan[18], Zihang Fang[19], Jingwei Li[20] & Brett A. Bryan[21], *"Future global urban water scarcity and potential solutions,"* Nature Communications, August 3, 2021, https://www.nature.com/articles/s41467-021-25026-3

[102] United States Environmental Protection Agency, *Basic Information about Source Water Protection,* https://www.epa.gov/sourcewaterprotection/basic-information-about-source-water-protection

---

11. https://www.nytimes.com/by/mira-rojanasakul

12. https://www.nytimes.com/by/christopher-flavelle

13. https://www.nytimes.com/by/blacki-migliozzi

14. https://www.nytimes.com/by/eli-murray

15. https://www.nature.com/articles/s41467-021-25026-3#auth-Chunyang-He

16. https://www.nature.com/articles/s41467-021-25026-3#auth-Zhifeng-Liu

17. https://www.nature.com/articles/s41467-021-25026-3#auth-Jianguo-Wu

18. https://www.nature.com/articles/s41467-021-25026-3#auth-Xinhao-Pan

19. https://www.nature.com/articles/s41467-021-25026-3#auth-Zihang-Fang

20. https://www.nature.com/articles/s41467-021-25026-3#auth-Jingwei-Li

21. https://www.nature.com/articles/s41467-021-25026-3#auth-Brett_A_-Bryan

[103] https://www.nynjbaykeeper.org/

[104] Monmouth University Uban Coast Institute, *Coastal Community Resilience Initiative,* https://www.monmouth.edu/uci/

[105] Billion Oyster Project, *Restoring Oyster Reefs to NY Harbor Through Public Education Initiatives,* https://www.billionoysterproject.org/home-1

[106] Friends of Liberty State Park, https://www.folsp.org/

[107] Chelsea Wald, *"Waste Not: A Brief History of the Urban Sewer System,"* Literary Hub, April 15, 2021,

https://lithub.com/waste-not-a-brief-history-of-the-urban-sewer-system/

[108] Kevin DeGood, *A Call to Action on Combating Nonpoint Source and Stormwater Pollution,* Center for American Progress, October 2020

[109] U.N. Environmental Programme, *"Turning off the Tap How the world can end plastic pollution and create a circular economy,"* May 26, 2023, p.xiv, https://www.unep.org/resources/turning-off-tap-end-plastic-pollution-create-circular-economy

[110] Science Direct, *"A review on microplastics and nanoplastics in the environment: Their occurrence, exposure routes, toxic studies, and potential effects on human health,"* Volume 181, August 2022, https://www.sciencedirect.com/science/article/pii/S0025326X22005148

[111] Mark O'Connell, *"What are the Plastic Particles in Our Bodies Doing to Us?"* Opinion, The New York Times, Sunday, April23, 2023, pp.6-7, https://www.nytimes.com/2023/04/20/opinion/microplastics-health-environment.html

[112] John Briley, *Confronting Ocean Plastic Pollution,* Pew Trusts, November 16, 2020, https://www.pewtrusts.org/en/trust/archive/fall-2020/confronting-ocean-plastic-pollution

[113] UN Environmental Programme, Intergovernmental Negotiating Committee on Plastic Pollution, March 2022, https://www.unep.org/inc-plastic-pollution

[114] UN Environmental Programme, Supra, pp.20-38

[115] Statista Research Department, "*Global plastic market size value 2021-2030,*" March 24, 2023, https://www.statista.com/statistics/1060583/global-market-value-of-plastic/

[116] Beyond Plastics and International Pollutants Elimination Network (IPEN) Report, *Chemical Recycling: A Dangerous Deception*, October 2023, https://www.beyondplastics.org/publications/chemical-recycling

[117] New EU rules to reduce, reuse, and recycle packaging packaging, European Parliament, April 24, 2014. www.europarl.europa.au[22]

[118] Erina Brown, Anna MacDonald, Steve and Deonie Allen *The potential for a plastic recycling facility to release microplastic pollution and possible filtration remediation effectiveness,* University of Strathclyde Glasgow, May 31, 2023

[119] Scientists Coalition for an Effective Plastics Treaty (2024), *Primary Plastic Polymers: Urgently needed upstream reduction.*

DOI: 10.5281/zenodo.10906376

[120] Food and Agriculture Organization of the United Nations, *The State of World Fisheries and Aquaculture 2022,* https://www.fao.org/documents/card/en?details=cc0461en

[121] Marcel Martinez-Porchas and Luis R. Martinez-Cordova, "*World Aquaculture: Environmental Impacts and Troubleshooting Alternatives,*" Scientific World Journal, 2012, https://www.ncbi.nlm.nih.gov/pmc/articles/PMC3353277/

[122] Marcel Martinez-Porchas and Luis R. Martinez-Cordova, Ibid.

[123] Tom Clynes, *From Sea to Table,* Environmental Defense Fund, Solutions, Vol.54, No. 4, Fall 2023, p. 6, https://vitalsigns.edf.org/story/sea-table

[124] Earth.org, *7 Solutions to Overfishing We Need Right Now,* February 22, 2023, https://earth.org/solutions-to-overfishing

[125] Christina Larson *"UN Ocean treaty talks resume with goal to save global biodiversity,* Associated Press, 2/19/2023, https://apnews.com/article/science-politics-international-agreements-climate-and-environment-united-nations-a1fc54e48fb875b759e1df1c147cc4a8

[126] William H. Westermeyer, *"How the Tea Party Transformed American Politics,"* February 17, 2017, sapiens.org/culture/tea-party-american-political-culture/

[127] Penelope Muse Abernathy, *The State of Local News 2023,* Northwestern University Medill School of Journalism, November 16, 2023, https://localnewsinitiative.northwestern.edu/projects/state-of-local-news/2023/report/#executive-summary

[128] Heather J. Williams, Alexandra T. Evans, Jamie Ryan, Erik E. Mueller, and Bryce Downing, *The Online Extremist Ecosystem*, Perspective, Rand Corporation, December 2021,

Williams and Evans, *How Extremism Operates Online,* Perspectives, Rand Corporation, April 2022, https://www.rand.org/pubs/perspectives/PEA1458-2.html

[129] Glenn Kessler, Salvadore Rizzo, and Meg Kelley, *Trump's false or misleading claims total 30,573 over 4 years,* The Washington Post, January 24, 2021, https://www.washingtonpost.com/politics/2021/01/24/trumps-false-or-misleading-claims-total-30573-over-four-years/

[130] Letter to Colonel Edward Carrington, January 16, 1787

[131] Bill Bradley, *We Can All Do Better,* Vanguard Press, 2012, p.4

[132] 521 US 844 (1997)

[133] Luke J. Matthews, Heather J. Williams, and Alexandra T. Evans, *Protecting Free Speech Compels Some Form of Social Media Regulation,* Commentary (The RAND Blog), October 20, 2023, https://www.rand.org/pubs/commentary/2023/10/protecting-free-speech-compels-some-form-of-social.html

[134] Daniel Oberhaus, *"Prepare for AI Hackers,"* Harvard Magazine, March-April 2023, p.12, https://www.harvardmagazine.com/2023/02/right-now-ai-hacking

[135] Melissa Heikkila, *Our quick guide to the six ways we can regulate AI,* MIT Technology Review, May 22,2023, https://www.technologyreview.com/2023/05/22/1073482/our-quick-guide-to-the-6-ways-we-can-regulate-ai/

[136] European Union, *Artificial Intelligence Act.,* 2023, https://www.europarl.europa.eu/RegData/etudes/BRIE/2021/698792/EPRS_BRI(2021)698792_EN.pdf

[137] The White House, *Executive Order on the Safe, Secure, and Trustworthy Development and Use of Artificial Intelligence,* October 30, 2023, whitehouse.gov/briefing-room/presidential-actions/2023/10/30/executive-order-on-the-safe-secure-and-trustworthy-development-and-use-of-artificial-intelligence/

[138] Joshua P. Melzer, *The US government should regulate AI if it wants to lead on international AI governance,* The Brookings Institution, Commentary, May 22,2023, https://www.brookings.edu/articles/the-us-government-should-regulate-ai/

[139] United States Surgeon General's Advisory, *Social Media and Youth Mental Health,* 2023, p.4, https://www.hhs.gov/sites/default/files/sg-youth-mental-health-social-media-advisory.pdf

[140] Kyooeun Jang, Lulia Jang and Nicol Turner Lee, *The fragmentation of online child safety regulations,* The Brookings Institution, Commentary, August 14, 2023, https://www.brookings.edu/articles/patchwork-protection-of-minors/

[141] New Jersey Senate Bill S-588, P.L 2022, c.138.

[142] Common Cause, *Combating Online Disinformation,* https://www.commoncause.org, Our Work

[143] Richard Andrews, *American Environmental Policy since 1964,* Oxford University Press, February 26, 2018 https://oxfordre.com/americanhistory/display/10.1093/acrefore/9780199329175.001.0001/acrefore-9780199329175-e-408

[144] John Adams, *"Thoughts on Government,"* 1776, https://constitutioncenter.org/media/files/6.5_Primary_Source__John_Adams%2C_Thoughts_on_Government_%281776

[145] Thomas Jefferson, *To the Republican Citizens of Washington County, Maryland,* March 31, 1809, https://founders.archives.gov/documents/Jefferson/03-01-02-0088

[146] Aristotle, *The Nichomachean Ethics,* 1101a10

[147] See Mortimer J. Adler, *We Hold These Truths,* Macmillan Publishing Co., 1987, p. 141

[148] GREGORY a. Smith, Michael rotolo and Patricia Tevington, *45% of Americans Say US Should be a "Christian" Nation,* Pew Research Center, October 27, 2022, pages 33, 43

[149] Virginia Bill of Rights, June 12,1776, article 16

[150] Thomas Jefferson, Letter to Charles Thomson on January 9, 1816,.

[151] Theodore Roosevelt, *The New Nationalism*, 1910, https://obamawhitehouse.archives.gov/blog/2011/12/06/archives-president-teddy-roosevelts-new-nationalism-speech

[152] President Franklin D. Roosevelt, January 11, 1944, State of the Union message to Congress

[153] President Harry Truman, Address to the National Association for the Advancement of Colored People (NAACP), June 19, 1947

[154] President Lyndon Johnson, Speech at the University of Michigan, May 22, 1964, https://www.presidency.ucsb.edu/documents/remarks-the-university-michigan

[155] Message from The President of the United States relative to Reorganization Plans Nos. 3 and 4 of 1970, https://archive.epa.gov/ocir/leglibrary/pdf/created.pdf

[156] President Barack Obama, *An Honest Government, A Hopeful Future,* University of Nairobi, Nairobi, Kenya, August 28, 2006, http://obamaspeeches.com/088-An-Honest-Government-A-Hopeful-Future-Obama-Speech.htm

[157] President Joseph Biden, *Inaugural Address,* January 20, 2021, https://br.usembassy.gov/inaugural-address-by-president-joseph-r-biden-jr/

[158] Letter of Thomas Jefferson to Isaac H. Tiffany, 1819

[159] Mortimer J. Adler, *Six Great Ideas,* Macmillan Publishing Co., 1981, pp. 138-139, 178-179, 195

[160] Greg Leiserson, Will McGrew, and Raksha Kopparam, *The Distribution of wealth in the United United States and implications for a net worth tax,* Washington Center for Equitable Growth, March 2019

[161] See Common Cause, *Our Work,* https://www.commoncause.org/our-work/; Brennan Center for Justice, *Democracy: An Election Agenda for Candidates, Activists, and Legislators,"* Solutions, 2018, https://www.brennancenter.org/our-work/policy-solutions/democracy-election-agenda-candidates-activists-and-legislators

[162] President Abraham Lincoln, The Gettysburg Address, November 19, 1863, https://www.abrahamlincolnonline.org/lincoln/speeches/gettysburg.htm

[163] Rebecca Winthrop[23], *"The need for civic education in 21st-century schools"*, Brookings Institute, June 4, 2020, https://www.brookings.edu/articles/the-need-for-civic-education-in-21st-century-schools/

[164] Letter to Colonel Charles Yancey, January 6, 1816, https://founders.archives.gov/documents/Jefferson/03-09-02-0209

[165] National Center for Education Statistics (NCES), *National Assessment of Educational Progress (NAEP) Report Card, 2022 Civics Assessment,* https://www.nationsreportcard.gov/highlights/civics/2022/

[166] Sarah Shapiro and Catherine Brown, *The State of Civics Education,* CAP20, February 21, 2018, https://www.americanprogress.org/article/state-civics-education/

[167] Papers of John Adams, Volume 1, V. *"A Dissertation on the Canon and the Feudal Law,"* No. 3, September 30, 1765, https://founders.archives.gov/documents/Adams/06-01-02-0052-0006

[168] Sarah Shapiro and Catherine Brown, *The State of Civics Education,* supra,

---

23. https://www.brookings.edu/experts/rebecca-winthrop/

INDEX

Milton Keynes UK
Ingram Content Group UK Ltd.
UKHW012052260524
443218UK00001BA/107